New Zealand

by Allan Edie

Allan Edie has worked in New Zealand
travel and tourism for over 35 years. For
a number of those years he was
Deputy Director General Services for
the New Zealand Automobile Association in
Auckland.Allan is well traveled and has written
four books and numerous magazine
articles about New Zealand.

Above: *Shotover Jet, Queenstown*

AA Publishing

Above: *Buskers in Cathedral Square, Christchurch*

Written by Allan Edie

First Published 1998. Reprinted Mar 1998. Reprinted Nov 1999. Reprinted 2001. Information verified and updated. Reprinted Apr 2002. **Reprinted 2004. Information verified and updated.** Reprinted March and Dec 2004

© Automobile Association Developments Limited 2004
Maps © Automobile Association Developments Limited 2003
Maps © 2001 Periplus Editions (Lower South Island).

Published by AA Publishing, a trading name of Automobile Association Developments Limited, whose registered office is Southwood East, Apollo Rise, Farnborough, Hampshire GU14 OJW. Registered number 1878835.

Automobile Association Developments Limited retains the copyright in the original edition © 1998 and in all subsequent editions, reprints and amendments.

A CIP catalogue record for this book is available from the British Library.

Find out more about AA Publishing and the wide range of travel publications and services the AA provides by visiting our website at www.theAA.com/bookshop

A02483

Color separation: BTB Digital Imaging, Whitchurch, Hampshire
Printed and bound in Italy by Printer Trento S.r.l.

Contents

About this Book

KEY TO SYMBOLS

Throughout the guide a few straightforward symbols are used to denote the following categories:

✚ map reference to the maps in the What to See section

✉ address or location

☎ telephone number

⊘ opening times

🍴 restaurant or café on premises or near by

🚌 nearest bus/tram route

🚉 nearest overground train station

🛥 ferry crossings and boat excursions

✈ travel by air

ℹ tourist information

♿ facilities for visitors with disabilities

✋ admission charge

↔ other places of interest near by

❓ other practical information

➤ indicates the page where you will find a fuller description

---

This book is divided into five sections to cover the most important aspects of your visit to New Zealand.

Viewing New Zealand pages 5–14
An introduction to New Zealand by the author.
   New Zealand's Features
   Essence of New Zealand
   The Shaping of New Zealand
   Peace and Quiet
   New Zealand's Famous

Top Ten pages 15–26
A selection of the Top Ten places in New Zealand, each with practical information.

What to See pages 27–90
The four main areas of New Zealand, each with its own brief introduction and an alphabetical listing of the main attractions.
   Practical information
   Snippets of 'Did You Know…' information
   4 suggested walks
   4 suggested tours
   2 features

Where To… pages 91–116
Detailed listings of the best places to eat, stay, shop, take the children and be entertained.

Practical Matters pages 117–24
A highly visual section containing essential travel information.

Maps

All map references are to the individual maps found in the What to See section of this guide.
For example, Aoraki/Mount Cook National Park has the reference ✚ 62B2 – indicating the page on which the map is located and the grid square in which the National Park is to be found. A list of the maps that have been used in this travel guide can be found in the index.

Prices

Where appropriate, an indication of the cost of an establishment is given by $ signs:
$$$** denotes higher prices, **$$** denotes average prices, while **$ denotes lower charges.

Star Ratings

Most of the places described in this book have been given a separate rating:
✪✪✪   Do not miss
✪✪   Highly recommended
✪   Worth seeing

Viewing New Zealand

Above: *Rainforest fern*
Right: *New Zealand
sheep*

Allan Edie's New Zealand

Early Travel
In the early 20th century, before the railway came through, the Whanganui River was promoted as "New Zealand's Rhine." Thus three days of river cruising, including a night spent on a houseboat miles from civilization, became a fashionable way to travel.

Mitre Peak rises up dramatically from Milford Sound, Fiordland's best-known attraction

According to tradition, the early Polynesian Maori peoples were the first human beings to inhabit New Zealand, traveling to the islands in fleets of canoes during the 10th to 14th centuries. They were followed by European explorers and merchants, and later, in the 19th century, settlers and soldiers, gold-diggers and opportunists arrived. Today, tourists come from all over the world.

Tourism New Zealand promotes the country as "100% Pure New Zealand," at "the most beautiful end of the Earth." To convince potential visitors that New Zealand is removed from the everyday hassles of the world; to explain that life here is how it used to be, and yet provide assurance that it is a thoroughly modern country with civilization never far away; and to convince them that, despite occupying such a tiny area on a world map, it offers a tremendous variety of scenery and attractions, requires some degree of marketing skill.

To live in one of the world's most desirable holiday destinations is my good fortune for, with its easy-going lifestyle, clean, uncrowded environment, and spectacular landscapes ranging from volcanoes to glaciers, New Zealand surely is a favored country.

New Zealand's Features

Petrified tree stumps litter the rock platform of Curio Bay in the Catlins region of the South Island

Time and Place
New Zealand lies in the temperate belt of the South Pacific Ocean; the 45th parallel (halfway between the Equator and the South Pole) passes through the South Island. In longitude it is almost exactly opposite the United Kingdom.

Standard time is 12 hours ahead of GMT; from early October until late March daylight-saving advances the time one hour.

Geography

The total area of New Zealand is 270,000sq km, of which two major islands, the North and South Islands, just 25km apart, comprise 98 percent. Although the South Island is a third larger than the North, the North claims three-quarters of the population – including the largest city, Auckland, with one million people, and the capital of Wellington. The South Island's leading city is Christchurch.

Stewart Island, 27km south of the South Island, is the third largest land-mass, covering about 1,700sq km.

No part of New Zealand is further than 130km from the sea. The coastline, 5,650km long, includes many islands, harbors and estuaries.

The Climate

Summer lasts from December to February and fine autumn weather usually lasts through to May. During the winter months of June to August there is more rain in much of the country and snow falls in the high country of both the North and South Islands.

The People

The total population is 4 million, nearly 80 percent of which is of European descent – mainly from Britain. The indigenous Polynesian people, known as Maori, comprise 15 percent. Other South Pacific peoples and Asians make up most of the balance. Over 80 percent of the population are urban dwellers.

Maori culture is evident throughout New Zealand: below, a carving from the Waitangi Meeting House, in Northland

Essence of New Zealand

The scenic beauty of New Zealand is well known. In many places the landscape is a dramatic mixture of mountains, glaciers, fiords, and turbulent rivers, yet, in contrast, there are also gentle fields of grass, evergreen forests, and quiet lakes. While for many visitors touring the countryside in a car or long-distance bus, or admiring the views through a window, glass in hand, is pleasure enough, over the past 20 years or so New Zealand has also become established as a destination for action, renowned for "soft" adventure and for more spectacular thrill experiences. Concern for the environment and a yearning for healthy pursuits has increased worldwide, making unspoilt New Zealand a popular destination for enjoying a host of outdoor activities.

White-water rafting near Rotorua, just one of the exciting sporting experiences New Zealand has to offer

THE **10** ESSENTIALS

*If you only have a short time to visit
New Zealand, or would like to get a really
complete picture of the country, here are the essentials:*

• **Take a bush walk** – there are many options ranging from 10-minute strolls in the native bush (indigenous forest) to one-week treks.

• **Visit a museum** – notable museums can be found in Auckland, Wellington, Christchurch and Dunedin, plus many other smaller towns.

• **Stroll along a beach** – West coast beaches can be wild at any season; safe swimming beaches abound in the rest of the country.

• **Climb a mountain** – choose alpine ranges, bush-clad hills, active volcanoes or suburban viewpoints.

• **Inspect a thermal area** – marvel at bubbling mud and spouting geysers, or swim in hot water pools. There are thermal spas in many parts of the North Island and two in the South.

• **Watch a Maori concert** – be charmed by the dances and songs of the indigenous Maori people. And maybe follow it with a *hangi* (▶ 95).

• **Ride a jet-boat** – fast rides

on rivers and lakes are just one of the country's many thrilling adventures.

• **Watch a rugby match, or go horse-racing** – both exemplify the sporting passion of New Zealanders.

• **Drink the local wine or beer** – try a chilled white wine, or an ice-cold beer: there are plenty of award-winning labels to choose from, and plenty of places to try them!

• **Eat a New Zealand delicacy** – special dishes include Bluff oysters, Nelson scallops, West Coast whitebait, Canterbury lamb and pavlova dessert.

Top: *the hot pools of the Waiotapu Thermal Reserve, near Rotorua*
Above: *Maori poi dancers.*

Weekend Flea-markets

Most cities now have a Saturday or Sunday flea-market where small traders sell fresh fruit and vegetables, crafts and sundry products. You can meet New Zealanders at their most casual. For starters, try Christ-church's Arts Centre, Nelson's Montgomery parking lot, Auckland's Otara Markets, and Avondale Racecourse.

The Shaping of New Zealand

Abel Tasman was attacked by Maori at Massacre Bay (Golden Bay) in 1642.

AD 950
The legendary Polynesian explorer Kupe discovers New Zealand.

1150
The approximate date for early Polynesian settlement.

1642
Dutchman Abel Tasman is the first known European to see New Zealand, but does not land.

1769
English navigator James Cook "rediscovers" New Zealand and returns on

Recognition of British sovereignty: Maori chiefs sign the Treaty of Waitangi

two more voyages. After him come whalers, sealers and merchants, who exploit the country and its Maori inhabitants.

1814
The first Christian missionary, Samuel Marsden, arrives. There are attempts to administer New Zealand from Australia.

1840
Captain Hobson, dispatched by the British government, arrives to initiate a treaty with the Maori and install British law. This Treaty of Waitangi still causes controversy today with its varying interpretations. Auckland was selected as the country's capital.

1861
Gold is discovered in Central Otago, and later on the West Coast of the South Island and around the Thames-Coromandel area.

1865
The capital is transferred from Auckland to Wellington.

1876
Having been temporarily established in 1867, Maori seats in Parliament were made permanent.

1882
First export of frozen meat to England. Supply of meat and wool to Britain becomes an essential component of the NZ economy.

1886
Mt Tarawera erupts, destroying three villages and the famous Pink and White Terraces.

1887
The central North Island volcanic peaks are given by Maori to the people of New Zealand and become the country's first national park.

1893
New Zealand women are the first in the world to vote in national elections.

1915
Gallipoli landings: New Zealand & Australian troops bond in battle and the ANZAC spirit is born.

1919
Women are permitted to stand for Parliament.

1928
The first aeroplane flight between New Zealand and Australia takes place.

1931
Hawkes Bay earthquake shatters the cities of Napier and Hastings, killing 256 people.

1935
The First Labour government introduces the Welfare State.

1936
Jack Lovelock wins New Zealand's first Olympic athletics gold medal in Berlin.

1953
The first tour of the

"This way for gold" early prospectors flocked to the town of Ross at the turn of the century

country by a reigning monarch, Queen Elizabeth II, takes place.

1970s
Mass market air travel paves the way for tourism to become major feature of New Zealand economy.

1981
South African rugby tour of New Zealand provokes violent anti-apartheid protests in main cities.

1990s
The Internet and technological revolution means that New Zealand's geographic isolation is less of an economic disadvantage.

1991
The Resource Management Act is passed, becoming the first environmental legislation of its kind in the world.

1996
The first national elections are held under the mixed-member proportional system, resulting in a new-style coalition government.

1997
Jenny Shipley becomes New Zealand's first woman prime minister.

2000
New Zealand's proximity to the International Date Line makes it one of the first countries in the world to usher in the new millennium.

11

Peace & Quiet

Noted British naturalist Dr David Bellamy has referred to New Zealand as "Moa's Ark" – the moa (now extinct) being one of the country's indigenous flightless birds and ark being a reference to the country's split from the supposed Gondwana super-continent, including Australia and Antarctica, some 80 million years ago.

A Land Apart

For millions of years, until the arrival of man about 1,000 years ago, New Zealand was isolated from the rest of the world and a unique collection of plants and animals was able to flourish undisturbed. Among these are the flightless birds which evolved because ground-dwelling mammals (their predators) had not reached New Zealand at the time of the split.

Man's presence, with the consequent agriculture and deforestation, has undoubtedly had a great impact on New Zealand's wildlife over the past few hundred years, but in spite of this a vast number of fascinating species has survived.

Guided walks can be taken on the spectacular Fox (below) and Franz Josef glaciers

A Protected Landscape

These days the natural landscape and its flora and fauna are well protected and New Zealand has 14 national parks, comprising over 3 million hectares – 11 percent of its land area. In addition there are three maritime parks, 20 forest parks, and nearly 4,000 other nature and scenic reserves.

Mountains rise to 3,754m. Indeed, three-quarters of the land area is above 200m. Glaciers, fiords, lakes, and rivers decorate the interior. The rich native evergreen forest provides splendid cover and the native birdlife population remains large, albeit reduced from yesteryear.

Some Specialties

The kiwi is New Zealand's best-known bird. It is both a symbol of the country and the name applied to its human residents. Unfortunately, its nocturnal nature, and reduced numbers, means that visitors rarely see it in its natural surroundings, although birds are kept at several zoos and aviaries.

The beautiful white herons return to their sole breeding colony each summer, near Whataroa in South Westland, where a special hide allows visitors to observe and photograph them. Yellow-eyed penguins and Fiordland crested penguins can be observed close-up at several South Island locations.

New Zealand's most famous flightless bird is the kiwi, although it is rarely seen in the wild and is now considered an endangered species

The tuatara survived the calamity that killed off the dinosaurs 65 million years ago. In the wild it is restricted to protected sanctuaries, but you can see this rare reptile at several museums. More accessible is the sea-life: go whale-watching at Kaikoura or swim with dolphins.

Enjoying and Conserving

Peace and quiet abounds in the New Zealand countryside. There are plenty of picnic sites away from the crowds and plenty of bush walks to either amble around in solitude or undertake with friends; there are rivers to fish and mountains to climb. Within an hour or so of wherever you are, there will be a choice of places to get away from it all.

An important facet of New Zealand tourism is its commitment to looking after the interests of visitors and the environment, and the conservation authorities do a credible job of managing this difficult relationship. While visitors are invited to enjoy the countryside, they are also asked not to exploit or destroy it.

New Zealand's Famous

National heroine Jean Batten, commemorated on a cigarette card

Father of Nuclear Physics
Scientist Ernest Rutherford, born near Nelson, went to Cambridge in England after studying at Canterbury College, now the University of Canterbury. The most famous achievement in his long and distinguished career was discovering how to split the atom. On his death in 1937 Rutherford was buried in Westminster Abbey, in London, having been knighted and made a peer.

Something So Strong
Singer-songwriter Neil Finn (1958–) joined his older brother Tim's band Split Enz before founding the even more successful Crowded House in 1985. The group enjoyed worldwide success into the 1990s with its albums, singles, and concerts. Finn's brilliantly crafted melodic songs have been likened to those of The Beatles, but his use of New Zealand idiom gives his sound its own distinctive edge.

Jean Batten (1909–82)
A world famous aviatrix, Batten became the first woman to fly solo from England to Australia, in 1934. In 1936 she was the first person to fly solo from England to New Zealand, taking 11 days.

Sir Peter Blake (1949–2001)
Born in Auckland, Sir Peter was renowned for his victories in the Whitbread round-the-world yacht race, his record-breaking trip around the world in a catamaran, and leadership of the America's Cup campaign, which New Zealand won in 1995, defended in 2000 and lost in 2003, after his tragic murder in Brazil.

Sir Edmund Hillary (1919–)
The country's most respected hero, Hillary was the first man to conquer Mount Everest (1953) and has been involved with other Himalayan and Antarctic expeditions.

Katherine Mansfield (1888–1923)
One of the 20th-century's greatest short-story writers, Mansfield located many of her fictions in Wellington and other New Zealand settings.

Arthur Lydiard (1917–)
Lydiard revolutionized endurance training in the 1950s and 1960s, coaching many athletes to Olympic medals. He also helped inspire the worldwide jogging phenomenon and introduced running for cardiac rehabilitation.

Dame Kiri Te Kanawa (1944–)
New Zealand's most famous soprano was born in Gisborne. Renowned as a leading international opera singer for more than three decades, Dame Kiri now performs regularly in New Zealand.

Top Ten

Above: *Surfers on Mt Maunganui beach*
Right: *Maori woodcarving, Rotorua*

15

1
Fiordland National Park

✚ 82A4

✉ At the end of SH94, north of Te Anau

☎ 03 249 8900 (Te Anau visitor information)

🕐 Tour coach to Milford Sound departs Te Anau 10:30AM; also 7:45AM in summer.

🍴 Hotel dining room and bistro at Milford ($$)

🚌 Day tours from Te Anau and Queenstown

⛴ Milford Sound: several launches daily (with meals on board)

✈ Scheduled and scenic flights from Queenstown to Milford Sound (☎ 03 442 4100)

♿ Good boardwalk at Milford Sound

✋ Free access

❓ Day tour from Queenstown (▶ 79)

Below: *the aptly named Mirror Lakes*

Fiordland National Park is not only the largest national park in New Zealand, but one of the largest in the world.

In contrast to the coastline at the north of the South Island, where the Marlborough Sounds offer a gentle landscape of bush-clad hills and meandering sea passages, the sounds of Fiordland National Park in the south are rugged, glacier-carved fiords with deep waters and precipitous sides. Inland, behind the jagged coastline, is an unspoiled region of bushy hills, deep lakes, and high mountains covering some 12,000sq km, where rare species of wildlife have managed to survive undisturbed. The high annual rainfall produces many dramatic waterfalls. The most northerly of the fiords is Milford Sound, and the road leading there is one of the scenic highlights of New Zealand. Don't be surprised in late spring if you drive through the remains of an avalanche. You can also fly to Milford, or walk the Milford Track (▶ 89) over four days. Most of the other fiords are inaccessible other than by

sea. A launch trip on Milford Sound is highly recommended and takes about two hours. The spectacle of the sheer cliffs rising 1,200m out of the water provides awesome photographic opportunities. Visit Milford Underwater Observatory for a fascinating glimpse of the unique ecology of the fiords. The trip to Doubtful Sound via Lake Manapouri (► 88) and the Wilmot Pass is also a must. Cruises of up to five days can be taken to some of the sounds. The gateway to Fiordland National Park is the township of Te Anau (► 90), situated beside Lake Te Anau (the South Island's largest lake).

Above: *a walking track follows the Hollyford Valley, the longest in Fiordland, to the coast at Martins Bay*

Left: *sheer rock walls define the edges of the Cleddau Valley*

17

2
Tongariro National Park

*Lake Rotoaira, at the
northern end of the park*

*This sacred "land of fire," given by Maori to the
New Zealand people over 100 years ago, is now a
Unesco World Heritage Area.*

✚ 51C4

✉ At the end of SH48, off
SH47 between SH1 and
SH4

☎ 07 892 3729
(Whakapapa visitor
information)

🕐 Year round (subject to
winter snow)

🍴 Grand Chateau ($$) is
the main hotel

🚌 Through National Park
and Ohakune

🚉 National Park and
Ohakune railroad
stations

♿ Few paths; accessible if
accompanied

✋ Free access

↔ Taupo (▶ 45)

❓ Ski tours in winter from
Auckland and
Wellington

Lying at the center of the North Island's volcanic plateau is
the island's highest mountain – the active volcanic peak of
Mount Ruapehu (2,797m). Adjacent to it are Mount
Ngauruhoe (2,291m) and Mount Tongariro (1,968m) and
together the trio form the heart of a high and sometimes
bleak area known as Tongariro National Park. The land was
given to the government by the Maori tribal owners in
1887, and it became New Zealand's first – and the world's
second – national park.

Tongariro is now New Zealand's most popular national
park, mainly because of its excellent ski areas. The
Whakapapa ski field lies on the northern slopes
of Mount Ruapehu (25km from a small community called
National Park), and the Turoa field is on the southwestern
slopes (served by the town of Ohakune). The ski season
generally runs from about late June to September –
sometimes longer.

Ruapehu is an active volcano with a warm crater lake
and although normally placid, there were eruptions in 1995
and 1996. Cone-shaped Ngauruhoe periodically emits a
cloud of steam, but rarely erupts. Tongariro is dormant, but
has a hot spring on its slopes.

There are many walking tracks through the park,
including the Tongariro Crossing, a popular full-day trek
across the shoulders of Mount Tongariro. For those fit
enough, it is possible to make a side trip to the top of
Tongariro, or even to Ngauruhoe.

3
Te Papa Tongarewa

Bold, imaginative, constantly changing and always fun, Te Papa is New Zealand's leading-edge national museum.

Te Papa is a bicultural museum and has a variety of exhibitions which tell the stories and display the *taonga* (treasures) of the Maori people, the discoverers of Aotearoa (New Zealand).

"Hands-on" exhibitions such as *Awesome Forces* and *Mountains to Sea* tell the stories of the formation of this land, and the creatures that live on it, while *Bush City* allows you to experience New Zealand's native bush right in the middle of the city.

The stories of New Zealand's immigrants are dramatically conveyed in *Passports*, while *Exhibiting Ourselves* shows how New Zealand portrayed itself to the rest of the world. *Golden Days* is a highly original attraction, where you can see 100 years of New Zealand history literally come alive in just 12 minutes – all inside a junk shop!

For those who enjoy a bit of a thrill, the *Time Warp* will delight you. The *Time Warp* features *Blastback* and *Future Rush*, which are exciting time-travel rides to the past and future, while virtual bungy-jumping, sheep shearing, and a variety of other classic Kiwi activities provide challenging interactive fun.

50A1

Cable Street, Wellington

04 381 7000

Fri–Wed 10–6; Thu 10–9

Food Train, ground floor near entrance ($); Icon restaurant ($$$); Espresso Bar ($$)

Good

General admission to Te Papa and most exhibitions free; charges apply for some special exhibitions, *Time Warp* virtual reality experiences and guided tours

Te Papa at night

4
Whakarewarewa Thermal Reserve

✚ 33D1

✉ Tryon Street (Thermal Reserve), Hemo Road (Arts & Crafts Institute)

☎ 07 348 9047

🕐 Daily 8–5 (winter), 8–6 (summer)

🍴 No dining in grounds

🚌 Minibus transfers from Rotorua visitor center

♿ Few; assistance required

✋ Moderate

↔ Rotorua (➤ 42)

❓ Guides available

The Prince of Wales Feathers geyser

If you can get to see only one attraction in the Rotorua region, then "Whaka" (as the reserve is commonly known) should be it.

The city of Rotorua (➤ 42), near the center of the North Island, is renowned for its volcanic activity evidenced by spouting geysers, bubbling mud, and a pervasive smell of hydrogen sulphide. The area is surrounded by forest, has a dormant volcano and over a dozen lakes, plus many other attractions. It is also a center for a display of Maori culture.

About 3km from the city center, Whakarewarewa is the most famous of Rotorua's five thermal areas. It features Pohutu (Maori for "splashing") geyser which spouts up 30m at regular intervals, and the smaller Prince of Wales Feathers geyser (reaching 12m), which always erupts first. Nearby are steaming cauldrons of bubbling mud and strange, moonscape-like silica formations.

Overlooking the thermal area of Whaka is a re-creation of a palisaded *pa*, or fortress, like the one used by Maori warriors in earlier days. Also close by is the New Zealand Maori Arts and Crafts Institute, established in the 1960s, where the cultural skills of the Maori people are demonstrated, and their work displayed. There is a souvenir shop and a concert of Maori action songs is presented daily at 12:15PM inside the Te Aronui a Rua Meeting House.

Close to the Whakarewarewa reserve is a grove of redwood trees, which offers a shady walk and provides a contrast to the many thousands of acres of pine trees that cover the "volcanic plateau" around Rotorua.

5
Abel Tasman National Park

Near the top of the South Island, this is neither New Zealand's largest nor grandest national park, but remains one of the most popular.

This park is named after the first known European to see New Zealand. It is less than an hour's drive northwest of Nelson city and its coastal location offers a refreshing and charming combination of native bush and golden sand beaches. It needs to be explored on foot as road access is limited.

The easy and very popular coastal track is one of the most beautiful in the country and takes two to three days to walk. Be sure to plan and watch out for tides if cutting across the lagoons. There are national park huts available for overnight stays and tickets should be purchased before setting out. Launches also serve the bays so walkers can tackle short sections if they wish.

Inland, the higher areas of the Park are more rugged, the landscape a mix of limestone and marble contours. Harwoods Hole at Canaan is the deepest known cave in the southern hemisphere.

There are two other national parks in the Nelson region. Kahurangi (► 72) in the northwest features the Heaphy Track, a good four-day hike, while Nelson Lakes National Park (► 74) to the south is known for the twin lakes of Rotoiti (where there is a visitor center) and Rotoroa. Surrounded by high mountains and dense forests, the park offers boating, trout fishing, bush walks, and, in the winter, skiing at the Rainbow and Mt Robert ski-fields. For the more experienced, there are demanding alpine climbs.

✚ 63E5

✉ Northwest of Nelson, via SH60

☎ 03 528 6543 (Motueka visitor information)

⊙ Year round

🍴 Awaroa Lodge ($$); no road access

🚌 Daily tour bus from Nelson

⛴ Ferries from Kaiteriteri and Nelson

♿ Few; not suitable

✋ Free access

❓ Reduced transport facilities in winter

Easy, level walking and lovely coastal scenery make Abel Tasman a favorite with hikers

6
Cape Reinga

🪦 32A5

✉️ Northern tip of the
North Island, via SH1

☎️ 09 408 0879 (Northland
Information Centre,
Kaitaia)

🕐 Year round

🍴 Waitiki Landing ($$);
18km from Cape

🚌 Daily tours from Kaitaia
& Paihia

♿ Good to viewpoint

✋ Free access

A lighthouse at Cape Reinga, New Zealand's northernmost accessible point, guards the merging waters of the Tasman Sea and the Pacific Ocean.

From the promontory there are panoramic views of the coast, which sweeps away in a combination of cliffs and sand-dunes. This is the departure point for the spirits of the Maori people returning to their legendary home of "Hawaiki." Part of the thrill of a visit to Cape Reinga is the journey there. It is 116km north of Kaitaia and 220km from Paihia, where most bus journeys depart. You can drive yourself, but one-day bus tours are popular as some include a 60km stretch along the misnamed Ninety Mile Beach on the western side of the peninsula. Rental vehicles are forbidden on this beach. Access at the northern end, connecting the beach with the road to the

Ninety Mile Beach (actually 90km) runs down the west side of the Northland peninsula

Cape, is via a stream-bed with quicksand and buses are the only vehicles permitted to cross here. Tours also stop at the Wagener Museum at Houhora, where there is a large collection of Victorian items and Maori exhibits. Next door is the Subritzky Homestead, an early pioneer house. You can mail a postcard from Cape Reinga, but there are few other facilities here to detract from the spectacular setting. More amenities are located 18km south at Waitiki Landing. Cape Reinga, it should be noted, is not in fact the most northerly point of New Zealand – that honor belongs to North Cape to the east – but it is as far north as you can easily get to, and has the advantage of being next to Ninety Mile Beach.

7

Queenstown's Skyline Gondola

One of the highlights of the South Island's premier tourist center is a ride high above the town on the Skyline Gondola.

The many attractions of Queenstown and its surrounding area are featured later in the book (➤ 79), but one of the most enjoyable things to do is to take a ride on the Skyline Gondola cableway, which opened in 1967. The commanding view from the hilltop makes this a good way to get your bearings. The base terminal is a 15-minute walk from Queenstown's shops.

The ride itself, lasting just four minutes, takes visitors 450m up a steep hillside in small gondolas suspended from overhead cables. From the viewing platform at the top of the hill the breathtaking views encompass Queenstown, Lake Wakatipu, and the surrounding snow-capped mountains of the Remarkables range.

The complex at the upper terminal includes a restaurant and a wide-screen cinema where an entertaining short film, *Kiwi Magic*, is shown at regular intervals throughout the day. The film takes viewers on a tour of New Zealand's finest scenery by various means of transport, including biplane and jet-boat.

82C4

✉ Brecon Street, Queenstown

☎ 03 441 0101

🕐 Daily 9AM–10PM

🍴 Café and restaurant morning to evening

♿ Check

✋ Moderate

↔ Arrowtown

❓ Queenstown (➤ 79)

The viewing platform on top of the Skyline Gondola cableway provides a great view of Queenstown

8

The TranzAlpine

 63D2

 Christchurch station, Addington

 0800 TRAINS (freephone)

 Depart 8:15PM, return arrival 6:05PM

 Refreshments available on train ($)

 Christchurch station; also Greymouth station

Few; assistance required

Expensive

Christchurch (➤ 64)

Crossing the Southern Alps via mountain passes, tunnels and viaducts, this single-track line links the east and west coasts of the South Island.

A success story of the privately operated rail system in New Zealand has been the promotion of the train from Christchurch, through the Southern Alps, to the West Coast town of Greymouth. The TranzAlpine has become a popular tourist service, as a one-way link between the coasts, and as a round-trip excursion from Christchurch. The narrow-gauge train is diesel-hauled and the carriages have large picture windows; there is also a carriage with open sides for viewing and photography.

Departing daily from Christchurch in the morning, the train crosses the neat and tidy farmlands of the Canterbury Plains, passing through a number of small towns before stopping at Springfield. From here the journey is spectacular as the train continues across viaducts and through tunnels across the Canterbury foothills up to Arthur's Pass. At 737m, this is the highest railroad station in the South Island and sees the arrival of many visitors bound for Arthur's Pass National Park, which offers numerous opportunities for hiking and mountaineering.

Shortly after leaving here the train enters the 8km Otira Tunnel for the descent of 259m to Otira. Now on the other side of the Alps, the rainforests and scrubby landscapes of Westland offer a contrast in scenery to the eastern side. The line continues past mountains and along river valleys before running alongside the Grey River into Greymouth. The train returns to Christchurch in the afternoon.

Approaching Arthur's Pass, the high point of the train journey through the Southern Alps

9
Aoraki/Mount Cook National Park

New Zealand's highest peak, Aoraki/Mount Cook, forms the centerpiece of this beautiful alpine area in the heart of the South Island.

Much of the South Island is mountainous and the Southern Alps mountain range forms a backbone for most of the island's length. Of some 220 named peaks over 2,300m in New Zealand, the highest, at 3,754m, commemorates a Maori mythical god and the gifted English navigator who first landed in New Zealand in 1769. Nearby, Mount Tasman is the second-highest peak, at 3,498m.

Aoraki/Mount Cook lies in the 70,000-hectare Aoraki/Mount Cook National Park, adjacent to Westland National Park. These two parks, together with Mount Aspiring (➤ 90) and Fiordland (➤ 16) national parks, have been incorporated into a World Heritage area.

Most of the alpine terrain of Aoraki/Mount Cook National Park is favored by trekkers and climbers. These mountains – two dozen of them exceeding 3,000m – offer a truly spectacular panorama of peaks, glaciers, and rivers from a number of tracks of varying difficulty. Full information is available from the park's visitor center. Flights in ski-equipped light aircraft are a popular option, taking in views of Aoraki/Mount Cook and the Alps, and including a landing on the snowfield of the Tasman Glacier. At 28km, it is the longest glacier in the world's temperate zones.

Most coach tours include Mount Cook village (also known as The Hermitage) on the itinerary, either looping in as a day trip, or spending a night or two.

🚩 62B2

✉ At the end of SH80, 333 km west of Christchurch

☎ 03 435 1818

🕐 Daily 8–6 (Mount Cook visitor information)

🍴 Dining facilities at Mount Cook hotels ($$)

🚌 Buses from Christchurch and Queenstown

♿ Few paths suitable

✋ Free access

Aoraki/Mount Cook rising up beyond Lake Pukaki, which is fed by the Tasman Glacier and the Tasman River

10
Waitomo Caves

32C1

On SH37, 8km off SH3, south of Otorohanga

07 878 8227

Daily, half-hourly, 9-5

Waitomo Hotel ($$)

Minibus transfers from intercity buses

Transfers from Otorohanga station

None

Expensive

Included in most North Island coach tours

Lighting brings to life the limestone formations of the Waitomo Caves

These are among New Zealand's most impressive natural wonders. Glow-worms twinkle like stars on the roof of a cave above an underground river.

The caves are situated some 200km south of Auckland, at the end of SH37 between the towns of Otorohanga and Te Kuiti. In the area are a number of rocky outcrops, with a labyrinth of caves and channels beneath. The two main caves open to the public are the Waitomo Caves and the Aranui Cave. The former, which have given their name to the area, are the more popular. Visitors in guided parties are led through subterranean chambers of varying sizes containing delicate limestone stalactite and stalagmite formations highlighted by special lighting effects.

The main feature of the Waitomo Caves, however, and the reason for their alternative name of the Glowworm Grotto, is the dinghy ride along an underground stream into a cave where, in the darkness, one can gaze up at thousands of glow-worms lighting up the roof like stars in the sky. The effect is created by the "lights" that these tiny insects create to lure prey into their mesh of sticky mucus threads.

The Aranui Cave is worth visiting for its beautiful limestone formations, although it does not have the attraction of glow-worms. Both caves are usually busy in the middle of the day with coach tours, so avoid this time if possible. Near the Waitomo Caves, the Museum of Caves has good audio-visual displays and shows about the glow-worms, while on the road leading to Waitomo the Ohaki Maori Village gives an interesting insight into the Maori culture and way of life. Except for a hotel, there are few facilities near the caves.

What To See

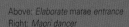

Above: *Elaborate marae entrance*
Right: *Maori dancer*

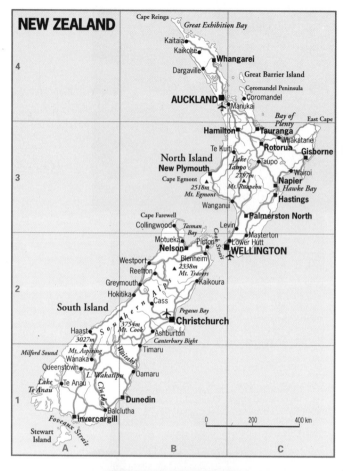

NEW ZEALAND

Cape Reinga
Great Exhibition Bay
Kaitaia
Kaikohe
Whangarei
Dargaville
Great Barrier Island
Coromandel Peninsula
AUCKLAND
Coromandel
Manukau
Bay of Plenty
East Cape
Hamilton
Tauranga
Whakatane
Te Kuiti
Rotorua
Gisborne
North Island
New Plymouth
Lake Taupo
Taupo
Cape Egmont
2518m
Mt. Egmont
2797m
Mt. Ruapehu
Wairoi
Napier
Hawke Bay
Hastings
Wanganui
Palmerston North
Cape Farewell
Levin
Collingwood
Tasman Bay
Masterton
Motueka
Picton
Lower Hutt
Nelson
WELLINGTON
Blenheim
Cook Strait
Westport
2338m
Reefton
Mt. Travers
Greymouth
Kaikoura
Hokitika
Southern Alps
Cass
South Island
Pegasus Bay
Christchurch
Haast
3754m
Mt. Cook
Ashburton
Canterbury Bight
Milford Sound
Mt. Aspiring
Waitaki
Timaru
Wanaka
Queenstown
L. Wakatipu
Oamaru
Lake Te Anau
Te Anau
Clutha
Dunedin
Balclutha
Invercargill
Foveaux Strait
Stewart Island

0   200   400 km

A   B   C

The terraced slopes of once-fortified Mount Eden, Auckland's highest volcanic peak, are still clearly visible

Upper North Island

This quarter of New Zealand, which includes the largest city, Auckland, has over half the country's population. In 1840, the country's founding document, The Treaty of Waitangi, was signed by Maori chiefs and representatives of the British Crown in the Bay of Islands. Near the northern tip of Northland is Cape Reinga, where Maori spirits of the deceased are said to depart for their ancient Polynesian home.

One hour east of Auckland is the Coromandel Peninsula, a delightful but rugged area of forest trails, old gold mines, deserted beaches, and the home of many craftspeople.

About three hours' drive southeast of Auckland is Rotorua, the center of traditional Maori culture and geothermal activity in a region of lakes, forests, and volcanic remnants. Further south, in the center of the North Island, is the resort town of Taupo, nestled on the shore of Lake Taupo with a distant view of the brooding volcanoes of magnificent Tongariro National Park.

"Auckland – Last,
loneliest, loveliest,
exquisite, apart"

RUDYARD KIPLING
The Song of the Cities
(1893)

Auckland

The city, built over the dormant remnants of some 50 volcanoes, sprawls across a narrow isthmus between the Pacific Ocean and the Tasman Sea, beach and bush readily at hand. With a population of 1 million, it is New Zealand's largest and most cosmopolitan city as well as being the main commercial and industrial center. Auckland also offers an array of cultural and sporting activities.

Auckland is the major New Zealand gateway for air and sea passengers and there are road, rail, and long-distance bus services to most parts of the North Island.

European settlement began here in 1840, and it was New Zealand's capital until 1865. The compact downtown area is still its hub, but there are major shopping and entertainment areas beyond the central streets, and the attractions for visitors spread to and beyond the suburbs.

Auckland's Harbour Bridge spans Waitemata Harbour

For those wanting to get away from the hustle and bustle of the city, in addition to its two harbors and gulf islands – the multitude of yachts always bobbing about in the Hauraki Gulf has given the city its nickname "City of Sails" – Auckland offers extensive regional reserves, a "new" volcanic island, a gannet colony, white and black sand beaches, and a forest backdrop to the west.

What to See in Auckland

ALBERT PARK ✪

Conveniently located close to downtown Auckland, this formal garden features a Victorian pavilion and statuary among its flowerbeds and trees. It is well used as a shady retreat by city office workers and students from the adjacent Auckland University campus.

✚ 36B2
✉ Princes Street
☎ 09 379 2020
🕐 Unrestricted
♿ Few
👋 Free access

AOTEA CENTRE ✪

Located on central Aotea Square, the building houses a visitor information bureau, a concert hall, a conference center, exhibition areas, restaurants, and bars. There is also a booking office for major Auckland events and concerts: check what's on during your stay.

The Auckland Town Hall, built in 1911, now serves as another concert venue. Also adjacent is the Entertainment Centre with its giant IMAX cinema screen.

✚ 36B2
✉ Aotea Square, Queen Street
☎ 09 309 2677
🕐 Daily 8:30–6
🍽 Alberts Restaurant ($$)
♿ Good

AUCKLAND HARBOUR BRIDGE ✪

Arching across Waitemata Harbour (➤ 38) to the North Shore suburbs, the bridge is over 1km long. It was opened in 1959 with four lanes and later widened to eight. Harbor cruises go under it and sightseeing buses go over it, but there is no pedestrian access – except for bridge-climbers and bungy-jumpers.

✚ 36B3
❓ Views from Shelly Beach Road and Westhaven Drive; beware of one-way streets

AUCKLAND ZOO ✪✪✪

Situated near the Museum of Transport, Technology and Social History (➤ 35), and connected to it by vintage tram, Auckland's zoo houses a selection of the usual overseas creatures plus native species such as the kiwi in a nocturnal house, and indigenous birds in a forest aviary. There is a farm animal section for children and Pridelands, which is a simulated African savannah enclosure featuring giraffes, zebras, and other animals. Auckland Zoo's endangered species program is internationally recognized.

✚ 36A2
✉ Motion Road, Western Springs
☎ 09 360 3819
🕐 Daily 9:30–5:30; last admission 4:15
🍽 Café ($)
🚌 045
♿ Good
👋 Moderate

Cape Reinga
Te Paki
North Cape
Great Exhibition Bay
Te Kao
Rangaunu Bay
Cape Karikari
Houhora
Doubtless Bay
Awanui
Mangonui
Kaitaia
Northland Forest Park
Kaeo
Bay of Islands
Cape Brett
Tauroa Pt
Waitangi Historic Reserve
Kerikeri
Russell
Okaihau
Paihia
Kaikohe
Kawakawa
Poor Knights Is
Hokianga Harbour
Omapere
NORTHLAND
Hikurangi
Matapouri
Waipoua Kauri Forest
Tutamoe Range
Wairoa
Ngunguru
Whangarei
Ruakaka
Hen & Chicken Islands
Dargaville
Waipu
Matakohe
Kauri Museum
Brynderwyn
Little Barrier Island
Kaipara Harbour
Wellsford
Warkworth
Kawau I
Waiwera
Hauraki
CENTRAL
Orewa
AUCKLAND
Hellensville
Whangaparaoa
Gulf
Muriwai Beach
AUCKLAND
Takapuna
Piha
Manukau
Waitakere Centennial Drive
Botanic Gardens
Papakura
Pukekohe
Waiuku
L Waikato
Waikato
Raglan
Hunt
SOUTH
Kawhia
Otorohanga
Waitomo Caves
Te Kuiti
Awakino
Mokau
North Taranaki Bight
Ahititi
Taumar

5

4

3

2

1

A   B   C

UPPER NORTH ISLAND

0 2 4 6 8 100 km

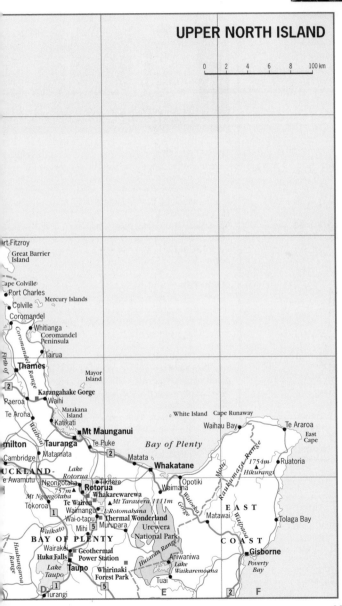

rt.Fitzroy
Great Barrier
Island
Cape Colville
Port Charles
Colville   Mercury Islands
Coromandel
Whitianga
Coromandel
Peninsula
Tairua
Thames
Mayor
Island
Karangahake Gorge
Paeroa   Waihi
Te Aroha   Matakana
Island
Katikati
Mt Maunganui
milton   **Tauranga**   Te Puke   *Bay of Plenty*   White Island   Cape Runaway
Cambridge   Matamata   Waihau Bay   Te Araroa
Matata   **Whakatane**   East
Cape
Lake
Rotorua   1754m   Ruatoria
UCKLAND   *Hikurangi*
e Awamutu   Ngongotaha   Tikitere   Opotiki
Mt Ngongotaha   **Rotorua**   Waimana
757m   Whakarewarewa   *Waioeka*   EAST
Tokoroa   Te Wairoa   *Mt Tarawera 1111m*   *Gorge*
Waimangu   *L.Rotomahana*   Matawai
Wai-o-tapu   **Thermal Wonderland**   Tolaga Bay
Mihi   Murupara   COAST
Waikato   Urewera
Wairakei   National Park
BAY OF PLENTY   Aniwaniwa   **Gisborne**
Huka Falls   **Geothermal**   *Lake*   *Poverty*
Power Station   *Waikaremoana*   *Bay*
Lake   **Taupo**   Whirinaki   Tuai
Taupo   Forest Park
Turangi
D   E   F

33

Once threatened with demolition, this handsome building standing on the edge of Albert Park now houses the City Art Gallery

CITY ART GALLERY ⚫⚫

Located within a Victorian edifice, the main gallery displays an important collection of New Zealand and imported paintings, prints, and drawings. Important touring displays from overseas also feature here (admission charge).

Opposite is the New Gallery (admission charge), an annex of contemporary art, and close by is the Auckland Central Public Library which houses a collection of historic and rare books.

🞖 36B2
✉ Corner of Wellesley and Kitchener streets
☎ 09 307 7700
🕐 Daily 10–5
🍴 Gallery café ($$)
♿ Good 👆 Free
❓ Free guided tour 2PM

DEVONPORT ⚫

Ten minutes across the harbour by ferry, the attractive North Shore suburb of Devonport has many 19th-century buildings housing cafés, bookshops, craft galleries, antique shops, and three museums.

🞖 36C3
✉ North Shore

DOMAIN AND AUCKLAND MUSEUM ⚫⚫⚫

The Domain's extensive parkland lies between downtown and Newmarket. The Winter Gardens display exotic plants in a hot-house and there is also a dell of New Zealand ferns.

Set in the Domain, the impressive Auckland Museum houses extensive displays of Maori and Polynesian cultures, the flora and fauna of New Zealand, arts and crafts from other countries, and a war memorial display. Special exhibitions are also frequently mounted.

🞖 36B2
✉ Auckland Domain
☎ Museum: 09 306 7067
🕐 Daily 10–5. Closed 25 Dec
♿ Few
👆 Free (charge for special exhibitions)
❓ Maori concerts 11AM, noon and 1:30PM daily, plus 2:30PM in summer

KELLY TARLTON'S ANTARCTIC ENCOUNTER ⚫⚫⚫
AND UNDERWATER WORLD

This popular "walk-in" aquarium has walk-through Plexiglass tunnels surrounded by fish and other marine animals, including sharks from the waters surrounding New Zealand.

There is also a ride through a re-creation of an Antarctic landscape, with a replica of explorer Sir Robert Scott's hut, a colony of live penguins, and an aquarium of life that exists below the Antarctic ice cap.

🞖 36C2
✉ Tamaki Drive, Okahu Bay
☎ 09 528 1994
🕐 Winter 9–6; summer 9AM–8PM
🍴 Kelly's café opposite ($$)
🚌 Nos 74- to 76-
♿ Few
👆 Expensive

MOUNT EDEN AND ONE TREE HILL ⊙⊙

Respectively the highest (196m) and second highest (183m) of Auckland's mainland volcanic peaks, both provide panoramic views, although Mount Eden gives the closer view of Auckland's downtown and harbor areas. Roads go to the top of both, but most sightseeing tours opt for Mount Eden. Both were former Maori *pa* (fortresses) and terracing and food storage pits are still visible.

	36B2/C1
⊠	Access off Hillside Crescent, Mount Eden Road
⊙	Unrestricted access
⫙	Langton's ($$), on slopes
⧠	Road to top
?	Road is one-way

MUSEUM OF TRANSPORT, TECHNOLOGY AND SOCIAL HISTORY ⊙

Known by its acronym "MOTAT," this museum, spread over two sites, displays vintage cars, aircraft, trams, colonial buildings, and other technological items from yesteryear, largely maintained by volunteer groups. Exhibits include a replica of the Pearse aircraft, which reputedly flew near Timaru earlier than the Wright Brothers' more famous flight; and the only Solent Mark IV flying boat left in the world. A historic tram runs to Auckland Zoo.

	36A2
⊠	Great North Road, Western Springs
☎	09 846 7020
⊙	Daily 10–5. Closed 25 Dec
⫙	Refreshments and restaurant ($$)
🚌	045
⧠	Good 🚋 Cheap
?	Working weekends advertised occasionally

NEW ZEALAND NATIONAL MARITIME MUSEUM ⊙⊙

As an island nation, New Zealand has a considerable maritime heritage and this is innovatively displayed inside old warehouses next to the waterfront near the foot of Queen Street. Exhibits range from Polynesian canoes to America's Cup yachts, and there are a number of workshops where crafts such as sail-making and wood-carving are demonstrated, trips on an old steam launch, plus the marina at the center of the complex where various craft are moored. Also shown is the importance of sea trade to the history and commerce of New Zealand.

	36B3
⊠	Hobson Wharf, Quay Street
☎	09 373 0800
⊙	Daily 9–6; 5 in winter
⧠	Few
🚋	Cheap

Above: *replica of Richard Pearse's first plane at MOTAT*

SKY TOWER ⊙⊙

The tallest structure in the southern hemisphere at 328m, the communications tower has three observation decks, a revolving restaurant and bar, and a glass floorplate for those unafraid of heights. At its base is the Sky City casino.

	36B2
⊠	Corner of Victoria and Federal Streets
☎	09 363 6422
⊙	Year round

35

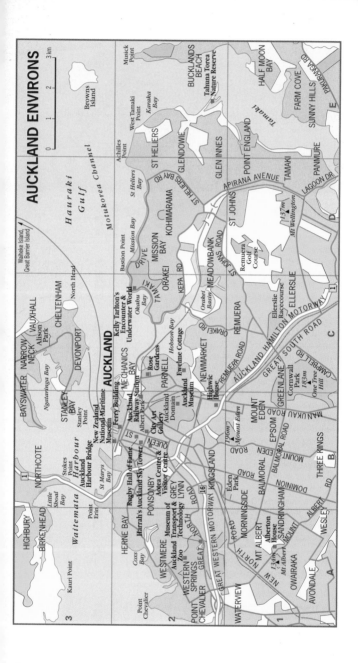

AUCKLAND ENVIRONS

A Walk Around Downtown Auckland

Attractions ranging from the Aotea Centre to a ride up the Sky Tower feature on this culturally interesting walk.

From Queen Elizabeth II Square walk eastwards along Customs Street then cross to Emily Place. Take the steps in the reserve to Princes Street, passing the Hyatt Regency Hotel.

Albert Park, a popular lunchtime retreat in the heart of the city

The Governor-General's former residence, the Maclaurin Chapel, and the Maidment Arts Theatre all form part of the extensive Auckland University.

Stroll through Albert Park (➤ 31) to the City Art Gallery (➤ 34).

A short block downhill is Queen Street. Note the Civic Theatre, opened in 1929; the Arabian designs inside are still eye-catching. It now forms part of the Entertainment Centre which includes the IMAX cinema. One block up Queen Street is Aotea Square. Cross the square to the Aotea Centre (➤ 31) and have a look within its atrium.

From the Aotea Centre, walk behind the Civic Theatre, along brick-surfaced Elliot Street, to Victoria Street, then turn left up hill.

Looming above you is the Sky Tower (➤ 35). Ride high to its observation decks to dine or admire the view.

Walk north along Federal Street and through St Patricks Square. Continue for one block west, then walk along Hobson Street to the water.

Ahead is the New Zealand National Maritime Museum and the America's Cup Village, built for New Zealand's defense of this trophy in 2000 and 2003. Enjoy a meal or a drink at one of the bars and cafés in this rejuvenated part of the city.

Distance
2.5km

Time
1 hour plus stops; suggest half a day

Start/end point
Queen Elizabeth II Square, at foot of Queen Street
🗺 36B2

Lunch
Cin Cin on Quay ($$)
✉ Ferry Building
☎ 09 307 6966

37

What to See Around Auckland

REGIONAL BOTANICAL GARDENS ✪✪

These 64-hectare gardens south of the city were created for educational and leisure purposes. Some 10,000 exotic and native plants found in the region are displayed and described. If you have limited time, visit Eden Garden, on the eastern flank of Mt Eden off Mountain Road in the city.

➕ 32C3
✉ Hill Road, Manurewa; 27km south of Auckland
☎ 09 267 1457 🕐 8–dusk
🍴 Café 💵 Free
♿ Good with assistance

WAITAKERE RANGES ✪✪✪

The forested hills to Auckland's west offer a scenic drive with bush scenery and views across the city. Signposted as Scenic Route 24, the drive starts at New Lynn and passes through Titirangi to Arataki Visitor Centre, where cantilevered platforms provide breathtaking views of the rainforest and Manukau Harbour. Inside the center are informative displays about the wildlife and plants of the area. You can also drive on to the beautiful ocean beaches of Piha, Karekare, Bethells (Te Henga), and Muriwai, where you can view a gannet colony close-up.

➕ 32C3
✉ Arataki Visitor Centre
☎ 09 817 0077
🕐 Daily 9–5 (Mon–Fri 10–4 in winter)
♿ Very good at visitor center
💵 Free

Maori carvings at the Arataki Visitor Centre

WAITEMATA HARBOUR AND HAURAKI GULF ✪

Waitemata Harbour, on the northern side of the isthmus, opens onto the Hauraki Gulf. You can get there by fast and frequent catamarans, ferries, launches, and yachts from the Ferry Terminal on Quay Street.

The most popular of the Gulf islands is Waiheke, 35 minutes from Auckland by fast ferry. Craft shops, vineyards, and superb beaches are among its numerous attractions.

The volcanic cone of Rangitoto is the nearest island to the city. The eruption that occurred here is the most recent in the region (thought to be sometime within the past 600 years). You can take a safari tour across the craggy rocks to the summit, or you can walk to the crater in about one hour.

➕ 36B3
✉ Ferry Building, Quay Street
☎ 09 367 9111
🕐 Call for cruise times
🍴 Cin Cin on Quay ($$) and Harbourside restaurant at wharf
♿ Few; should be accompanied
💵 Cruise prices vary

A Drive Through Suburban Auckland

Starting from the Ferry Building on Quay Street, the drive heads east around the bays of Tamaki Drive to St Heliers, then loops inland to the suburbs of Remuera and Newmarket before returning via Parnell to Quay Street.

Tamaki Drive passes the public Parnell Swimming Baths and Okahu Bay. Kelly Tarlton's Antarctic Encounter and Underwater World (➤ 35) is a worthwhile stop.

Continue to Mission Bay, a popular swimming beach and an area of busy cafés. A short walk to the Bastion Point headland provides vistas of the harbor and Gulf. Drive on to Kohimarama and the waterfront village of St Heliers.

Turn right onto St Heliers Bay Road, follow this up the hill to the St Johns Road traffic lights, where you turn left into St Johns Road, then right at the traffic circle.

This leads to Remuera Road and through the wealthy suburb of Remuera, to the fashionable entertainment and shopping center of Newmarket. Turn right on Broadway and continue straight on to Parnell Road. Domain Drive on your left leads to the Domain and Auckland Museum.

You could take a one-hour stroll down Parnell Road, parking if possible near the Anglican Cathedral at the top of the road. The area around the colonial-style Parnell Village has many restaurants, cafés, crafts shops, and boutiques.

Continue driving, turning right just past the Cathedral into St. Stephens Avenue and turn left into Gladstone Road. Pause for a fragrant breather at the Rose Gardens and another view of the harbor before returning to the Ferry Building.

Distance
24km

Time
1 hour plus stops; suggest at least half a day

Start/end point
Ferry Building, Quay Street
✚ 36B3

Lunch
Saints Waterfront Brasserie ($$)
✉ 425 Tamaki Drive, St Heliers
☎ 09 575 9969

The Auckland Museum houses fascinating displays of Maori and Polynesian culture and the natural history of New Zealand, including dinosaurs and other extinct species.

Bay of Islands

In addition to being one of New Zealand's most historically interesting regions (for both European and Maori), this is among the North Island's most popular resort areas. The Bay of Islands Maritime and Historic Park consists of over 800km of coastline and some 150 islands, as well as many reserves on the surrounding mainland and the communities of Paihia, Russell, and Kerikeri.

Bay of Islands attracts visitors in their hundreds

➕ 32B4
✉ Kemp House and Stone Store: Kerikeri Basin, Landings Road
☎ 09 407 9236
🕐 May-Oct 10-4; Nov-Apr 10-5. Closed 25 Dec
♿ Few; ground floor only
👜 Cheap

➕ 32B4
✉ Paihia wharf: Marsden Road

CAPE REINGA (➤ 22, TOP TEN)

KERIKERI　　　😊😊

Kerikeri, situated 23km from Paihia, is known for its citrus fruit orchards and craft workshops. It is the small harbor basin, however, that is of most interest. Historic sites here include **Kemp House**, erected in 1822 as the country's second mission station, now the oldest surviving building in New Zealand, and the **Stone Store**, originally part of the mission settlement but now a museum.

Across the inlet is Rewa's Maori Village, a full-size reconstruction of a pre-European Maori fishing village.

PAIHIA　　　😊

Paihia, the tourist base of the Bay of Islands, sprawls over three bays. Its town center is the wharf, from where various scenic cruises depart, as well as a regular passenger service across to Russell (➤ 41). Accommodations, restaurants, and cafés are plentiful.

From the southern end of Paihia, the Opua-Paihia Coastal Walkway is an attractive 5.8km walk – allow about 2–3 hours each way. The scenery includes sandy beaches and mangrove boardwalks. Adjacent to the walkway is Harrison Scenic Reserve, one of the best examples of coastal forest in the area.

RUSSELL ✪✪

Russell, New Zealand's first European settlement, was known as "the hell-hole of the Pacific" back in the days when lawless whalers came into violent contact with local Maori. The town is now a quiet hamlet, although the bullet holes in the wooden church (built in 1836) and the graves in its churchyard testify to its colorful past.

Other sights include **Pompallier** (built by the first Catholic bishop), and nearby Flagstaff Hill – scene of disputes between British troops and local Maori in the 1840s.

The **Captain Cook Memorial Museum** includes a one-fifth scale model of Cook's ship, *Endeavour*.

🚩 32C4

Pompallier
✉ The Strand
☎ 09 403 7861
🕐 Dec–Apr daily 10–5;
   May–Nov guided tours
🎟 Cheap

Captain Cook Memorial Museum
✉ York Street
☎ 09 403 7701
🕐 Daily 10–4 (Jan 10–5)
🎟 Cheap

WAIPOUA KAURI FOREST ✪✪

This stand of forest is a remnant of the bush that once covered nearly all the Northland region. New Zealand kauri is one of the world's oldest growing and largest trees, with a long straight trunk; its golden timber was highly prized, and its gum used as a resin. The scenic road through the reserve passes many of these trees, but the largest, called "Tane Mahuta," requires a short bush walk.

🚩 32B4
✉ SH12; 112km from Paihia
☎ 09 439 8360 (Dargaville
   visitor information)
🕐 Unrestricted access
🎟 Free

WAITANGI HISTORIC RESERVE ✪✪

Just north of Paihia is the Waitangi Historic Reserve, where, in 1840, a treaty was signed by Maori chiefs and the British Crown under the auspices of Captain (later Governor) Hobson. The treaty promised the Maori people certain rights in exchange for British sovereignty, but its interpretation remains controversial today.

The Treaty House, built in 1834 as a home for the British government representative, is open as an exhibit. The Waitangi grounds also display a centennial (1940) Maori Meeting House, and a 36m Maori *waka* (canoe).

🚩 32B4
✉ Tau Henare Drive, near
   Paihia
☎ 09 402 7437
🕐 Daily 9–5 winter;
   9–6 summer
🍴 Copthorne Hotel &
   Resort Bay of Islands ($$)
♿ Good if accompanied
🎟 Cheap

Waka (war canoe)

Rotorua

The city of Rotorua, 234km southeast of Auckland, is recognized as the North Island's leading tourist center because of its Maori culture, geothermal activity, and scenic variety. The volcanic activity is first apparent because of the sulfureous odors in the air.

Whakarewarewa (► 20) is the city's leading geothermal reserve, but the area has a number of other places with such activity, plus a dozen lakes, an evergreen forest, and a host of other attractions. A selection is listed here.

The visitor information center is in Fenton Street and the main shopping thoroughfare is Tutanekai Street.

A sheep-shearing demonstration at Rotorua Agrodome

🕂 33D1
✉ Western Road, Ngongotaha
☎ 07 357 1050
🕐 Shows three times daily from 9:30. Open 365 days
♿ Good 🍴 Moderate

AGRODOME ✪✪

Here the story of sheep in the New Zealand economy is told with regular displays of sheep-shearing, plus lamb feeding, mock sheep auctions, and sheep and cattle shows. Several varieties of sheep are on view and tours of the farm are available. There is also a chocolate factory and a woolen goods shop.

🕂 33D1
✉ SH30, Tikitere; 18km from Rotorua
☎ 07 345 3151
🕐 Daily 8:30–5
♿ Good 🍴 Cheap

HELL'S GATE ✪✪

The reserve here covers about 10ha and an extensive walk takes visitors past pools of hot water, bubbling mud, and other features. Irish playwright George Bernard Shaw is supposed to have given the area its name by exclaiming "Hell's Gate!" on first seeing it.

🕂 33D2
✉ Memorial Drive, foot of Tutanekai Street
☎ 07 348 6634 (Lakeland Queen cruise)
🕐 Two or three cruises daily
♿ Good 🍴 Moderate

LAKE ROTORUA ✪

This is the largest of a dozen or so lakes in the area. The waterfront area is a pleasant site where several lake cruises on different kinds of craft are available.

Mokoia Island, in the middle of the lake, is the setting for a popular Maori legend about two young lovers called Hinemoa and Tutanekai; you can visit the island.

Tudor-style St Faith's Church at the Maori village of Ohinemutu

Did you know ?

There are several places in Rotorua where concerts of Maori dance and song are performed daily. Tamaki Tours (► 113) operate an evening tour combining a concert and a hangi (► 95) in a forest setting that offers a first-hand Maori cultural experience.

OHINEMUTU ✪

Ohinemutu, a Maori village on the shore of Lake Rotorua, was once the lake's main settlement. It remains of interest with its Anglican St Faith's Church (notice in particular the window showing Christ dressed in a Maori cloak), and a carved Maori meeting house.

⊠ Mataiwhera Street
☎ 07 348 5179 (Rotorua visitor information)
🕐 Daily 9–4:30 ♿ Few
💷 Free, or donation

RAINBOW SPRINGS ✪✪✪

Rainbow and Fairy Springs, combined as one attraction, are sites where natural freshwater gushes from the ground. There are pools of giant trout amid bush and ferns. Rainbow Farm Park, opposite Rainbow Springs, displays an array of New Zealand farm animals, including sheep and cows. There are sheep-shearing, cow-milking, and sheep-dog displays, and there is also a souvenir shop.

⊠ Rainbow Springs: Fairy Springs Road
☎ 07 347 9301
🕐 Daily 8–5
♿ Good
💷 Moderate

SKYLINE SKYRIDE ✪✪

Mount Ngongotaha (757m) is a prominent peak on the western shore of Lake Rotorua. Although there is a road to the top, the Skyride gondola is a popular attraction, taking passengers up 200m to a viewpoint halfway up the mountain, from where there is a panorama of the city and lake. An alternative way back down is by luge (a sled following a purpose-built track). There is a restaurant at the top of the gondola and a herb shop at its foot.

🎫 33D1
⊠ Fairy Springs Road
☎ 07 347 0027
🕐 Daily 9–restaurant closing
🍴 Skyline restaurant
♿ Few
💷 Moderate

43

TE WAIROA BURIED VILLAGE ⭐⭐

In 1886 the dormant volcano of Mount Tarawera erupted, resulting in loss of life and the burying of three villages – Te Wairoa, Moura, and Te Ariki – beneath several feet of lava and mud.

Also obliterated were the famous Pink and White Terraces, fan-like natural silica formations on the shores of Lake Rotomahana, which had been an early tourist draw for the region. The village of Te Wairoa has since been partly excavated, and may be seen separately or as part of a round-trip incorporating other local sites. A small gallery displays "before and after" pictures.

Tours of the volcano can be taken from Rotorua's visitor center in Fenton Street.

WAIMANGU ⭐⭐

Waimangu is another area with impressive volcanic activity. There is a walk past thermal pools, including a boiling 4ha lake, and a path leads down to Lake Rotomahana where lake cruises sail past steaming cliffs, and over the sunken site of the Pink and White Terraces (▶ above). A round-trip tour with a short bush walk links this lake with Lake Tarawera, returning to Rotorua via Te Wairoa Buried Village (▶ above).

WAI-O-TAPU THERMAL WONDERLAND ⭐⭐

The most colorful of the geothermal areas, Wai-o-tapu features thermal zones that have been given their different hues by mineral deposits. Highlights include the Lady Knox Geyser, which plays every morning (primed with the help of soap) at 10:15 and can reach heights of 20m, and the hot Champagne Pool.

WHAKAREWAREWA THERMAL RESERVE (▶20, TOP TEN)

🔲 33D1
✉ Tarawera Road; 14km from Rotorua
☎ 07 362 8287
🕐 Nov–Mar daily 8:30–5:30; Apr–Oct 9–4:30
🚌 Tour bus available
♿ Good on upper paths; waterfall track unsuitable
🍴 Moderate

🔲 33D1
✉ Off SH5; 19km south of Rotorua
☎ 07 366 6137
🕐 Daily 8:30–5
🚌 Tour bus available
♿ Good if accompanied; site on an incline
🍴 Moderate

🔲 33D1
✉ Off SH5; 32km south of Rotorua
☎ 07 366 6333
🕐 Daily 8:30–5 (later Jan–Feb)
🚌 Tour bus available
♿ Good 🍴 Moderate

The Champagne Pool

Taupo

The town of Taupo nestles at the heart of the North Island beside Lake Taupo, looking out towards the distant peaks of the Tongariro National Park. Together with the surrounding area, it has become a major holiday center and offers the visitor a wealth of attractions.

HUKA FALLS ⭐⭐

Near Wairakei, where the Waikato River plunges over an 11m drop, are the Huka Falls. Though not high, the huge volume of water that crashes through this narrow defile makes it a thunderous spectacle. There are various vantage points along the path.

🕂 33D1
✉ Off SH1; 7km north of Taupo
☎ 07 376 0027 (information)
🕐 Unrestricted access
♿ Good 🎟 Free

The calm waters of Lake Taupo

LAKE TAUPO ⭐

Formed thousands of years ago by a series of volcanic upheavals, Lake Taupo, covering 600sq km, is the largest lake in New Zealand.

The lake is internationally renowned for its trout fishing, and fishing guides and charter boats are available. There are also cruises on the lake and along parts of the Waikato River, New Zealand's longest waterway, which flows out of the lake.

🕂 33D1
✉ Taupo visitor information: Tongariro Street
☎ 07 376 0027
🕐 Daily 8–6
🚢 Lake cruises depart from Redoubt Road
🎟 Cruise prices vary

WAIPAHIHI BOTANICAL GARDENS ⭐⭐

This is an extensive drive-through reserve with walks lined with many species of native trees, and beds of rhododendrons and azaleas. The gardens are at their best when the shrubs are in full flower during October.

🕂 33D1
✉ Shepherd Road, Taupo
☎ 07 378 7293
🕐 Open daylight hours
♿ Good 🎟 Free

WAIRAKEI GEOTHERMAL POWER STATION ⭐⭐

The visitor center shows how the geothermal steam is harnessed to generate electricity. Nearby there is a lookout over the geothermal field.

Wairakei Thermal Valley and Craters of the Moon are other areas of geothermal activity, both featuring steaming vents and bubbling mud pools. The first has an admission fee, the second is free. Both require extensive walking.

🕂 33D1
✉ SH1; 10km north of Taupo
☎ 07 378 0913
🕐 Daily 9–4:30
🍴 Wairakei Resort
♿ Good at visitor center
🎟 Free displays

In the Know

If you have only a short time to visit New Zealand, or would like to get a real flavor of the country, here are some ideas:

Above and below: two aspects of traditional New Zealand life – family picnics on the beach and a greeting Maori warrior-style

10
Ways To Be A "Kiwi"

Love sport, follow sport, talk about sport, maybe even have a go at it.
Have a weekend picnic, or enjoy a barbecue at the beach, or anywhere, just go!
Go to the bush, or the river, or the mountain.
Travel by car (driving on the left!) or 4WD most places. Bikes are for the energetic: what a splendid way to see the country!
Have lunch at a café and make new Kiwi friends.
Watch an All Blacks rugby game and see why they are national heroes.

Don't discuss religion but do discuss politicians – blame everything bad on them.
"Shout" a Kiwi a beer. A friendly way to thank Kiwis is to "shout" them (or buy them) a drink.
Don't talk between 8:00 and 8:05 on Saturday night. That's when the national Lotto is drawn.
Slap on the sunscreen. Your skin can burn extremely quickly in the fierce summer sun here.

10
Places To Have Lunch

Bell Pepper Blues ($$)
✉ 474 Princes Street, Dunedin ☎ 03 474 0973. Modern interesting selection.
Boulcott Street Bistro ($$) ✉ 99 Boulcott Street, Wellington ☎ 04

499 4199. International bistro selections.

Chocolate Fish Café ($$) ✉ 497a Karaka Bay Road, Scorching Bay ☎ 04 388 2808. Favourite beachside haunt of the *Lord of the Rings* stars (➤ 94).

Cin Cin on Quay ($$) ✉ 99 Quay Street, Auckland ☎ 09 307 6966. Busy waterfront café.

Crown Plaza ($$) ✉ Corner Kilmore & Durham streets, Christchurch ☎ 03 365 7799. Light and elegant in this hotel atrium.

Gibbston Valley Winery ($$) ✉ Queenstown–Cromwell SH6 (24km from Queenstown) ☎ 03 442 6910. Light lunches in a southern vineyard.

Iguaçu ($$) ✉ 269 Parnell Road, Auckland ☎ 09 358 4804. Trendy cuisine.

one red dog ($$) ✉ 151 Ponsonby Road, Auckland ☎ 09 360 1068. The best pizzas in Ponsonby.

Palazzo del Marinaio ($$) ✉ Shades Arcade, City Mall, Cashel Street, Christchurch ☎ 03 365 4640. Seafood and other dishes.

The Portage Hotel ($$) ✉ Beachcomber Cruises, Picton ☎ 03 573 4309. A launch cruise and views.

10
Top Activities

Bird-watching: from November through to February take a tour to see white herons roost near Whataroa in Westland.

Four-wheel-drive Safari: follow an old stage-coach road on the Dunstan Trail, out of Alexandra.

Bungy jumping

Just Looking: Kelly Tarlton's Antarctic Experience and Underwater World, in Auckland.

Golfing: there are over 300 courses!

Maori Experience: visit a *marae* or eat a *hangi*.

Swimming: brilliant beaches, rivers and lakes everywhere

Skiing: try Coronet Peak, near Queenstown.

Trout Fishing: open season year-round at Taupo.

Walking: from Arataki Visitor Centre in Auckland's Waitakere Ranges for an experience of the New Zealand bush.

Wine Trail: tour the Marlborough vineyards.

White-water canoeing

10
Adventure Activities

Big game fishing: Bay of Islands.

Bungy-jumping: Queenstown.

Canoeing: Whanganui River.

Glacier walking: Fox Glacier.

Hang gliding: around Queenstown.

Horse riding: Arrowtown's old gold-mining trail.

Hunting: Taupo's Kaimanawa Ranges.

Jet-boating: Queenstown's Shotover River jet-boat.

White-water rafting: Try Wairoa River near Tauranga.

Wilderness walking: the Whirinaki Forest; Milford Track.

Lower North Island

South of Lake Taupo the North Island becomes hillier. Tongariro National Park, the first of New Zealand's national parks, is dominated by a trio of volcanoes, marking the southern edge of the volcanic belt.

In the west, the city of New Plymouth is watched over by its dormant volcano, Mount Taranaki. In the east, the hills of Hawkes Bay, a horticultural, wine-growing, and sheep-farming region, sweep down to the twin cities of Napier and Hastings. In between, the navigable Whanganui River is steeped in Maori history, and you can canoe most of its 329km. Down at the southern tip of the island lies the vibrant capital city of Wellington, guarding Cook Strait.

Within easy reach of the capital is the Wairarapa, where the small town of Martinborough has several boutique wineries. Beyond, a road leads to Palliser Bay and Cape Palliser, where there are rugged, remote beaches.

"In this nasty, overcrowded and polluted world, New Zealand is as near to a people's paradise as fallible humanity is likely to get"

AUSTIN MITCHELL
The Half-Gallon Quarter Acre Pavlova Paradise (1972)

Ride the Wellington cable car for great views of the city

Wellington

European settlement commenced here in 1840 and, following its selection as New Zealand's capital in 1865, the city has never looked back.

Located at the southern tip of the North Island, Wellington is an important commercial center and has excellent transport links with the rest of the country – by ferry, air, rail, and long-distance bus. It is also the nation's cultural center, home town of the New Zealand Symphony Orchestra, the Royal New Zealand Ballet Company, and Te Papa Tongarewa, the Museum of New Zealand. Various music and arts festivals are held here each year, and the entertainment scene is thriving. Bounded on three sides by the sea and inland by circling hills, Wellington is a compact city, easy to get around on foot, and its fine deep harbor acts as a focal point. To provide relief from the hustle and bustle, there are plenty of gardens, parks and hilly viewpoints, in addition to the nearby beaches.

It is a city with character, divided into several parts. There is the older, distinctive heart, including its parliament and government offices; adjacent is the Hutt Valley – largely residential, but with industry at its southern end; and there are the northern satellite city of Porirua and the long sandy beaches of the Kapiti Coast.

Opposite: *informal street life in Wellington*
Above: *the face of the modern city*

51

What to See in Wellington

BOTANIC GARDEN

Spread over 25ha, this landscaped garden includes both native bush and exotic plants, and there is also a tulip display each spring. The Lady Norwood Rose Garden with more than 100 different species of rose and a Begonia House are additional features.

At the top of the hill (near the top cable-car terminal) is the Carter Observatory, with a planetarium, astronomy displays, and a hands-on area.

🔲 50B1
✉ Tinakori Road, Glenmore Street & Upland Road
☎ 04 801 3071
🕐 Unrestricted access
🚋 Cable car
♿ Few; slopes and steps in parts
🖐 Free

CABLE CAR 🟢🟢

Rising from the terminal off Lambton Quay, Wellington's main shopping street, the cable cars climb a 1-in-5 gradient to Kelburn. The service began in 1902, but the original wooden cable cars have been replaced. At the top, where there are fine views of the harbor and city, is the upper entrance to the Botanic Garden (► above), providing an alternative walking route back down (► 53).

🔲 50B1
✉ Cable Car Lane, off Lambton Quay
☎ 04 801 7000 (Ridewell timetable enquiries)
🕐 7AM (Sat & Sun 9AM)–10PM
♿ None; assistance required
🖐 Cheap

The birthplace of renowned author Katherine Mansfield

KATHERINE MANSFIELD BIRTHPLACE 🟢

New Zealand's greatest short-story writer was born in this wooden house in 1888. Now restored and furnished appropriately for the period, the building is open for viewing and has permament and changing exhibitions. The garden has been laid out in its original Victorian design.

🔲 50B1
✉ 25 Tinakori Road
☎ 04 473 7268
🕐 Daily 10–4
♿ Few; assistance required
🖐 Cheap

MUSEUM OF WELLINGTON CITY AND SEA 🟢🟢

Displays featuring the history of Wellington Harbour, over 80 model ships, nautical paraphernalia, old photos, and lots more, illustrate the long maritime associations of the region. The museum is housed in the old Harbour Board building (1891) on Queens Wharf.

🔲 50B1
✉ Queens Wharf
☎ 04 472 8904
🕐 Daily 10–6 (earlier closing in winter)
♿ Few 🖐 Cheap

A Walk Around Wellington

An extra dimension is given to this walk by first taking a breathtaking ride on the cable car (➤ 52) from its terminus in Cable Car Lane, off Lambton Quay, up past Victoria University to the Kelburn terminus. From here on it's all downhill.

After alighting from the cable car, go to the look-out points to admire the city and harbor views.

Immediately adjacent is the upper entrance to the Botanic Garden (➤ 52). Follow any of the paths downhill through native bush to the Lady Norwood Rose Garden.

At the bottom, continue around Anderson Park then go through Bolton Street Memorial Park, carry on over the freeway and after that go down to Bowen Street.

Stroll through the grounds of parliament, passing the Beehive, Parliament House, and the Parliamentary Library buildings. Exit onto Molesworth Street and cross over to the National Library, which includes the Alexander Turnbull Library (➤ 54).

Continue walking up Molesworth Street, then turn right into Pipitea Street to reach Mulgrave Street.

Here you can take the opportunity to visit Old St Paul's Church (➤ 54), and admire its interior design and decoration.

Carry on down Mulgrave Street past the railroad station to Queens Wharf and reward yourself with a coffee or wine at one of the waterfront cafés before returning to Cable Car Lane.

Distance
2.5km walk

Time
1.5 hours plus stops

Start/end point
Cable Car Lane, off Lambton Quay
✚ 50B1

Lunch
Café at the National Library ($)
✉ 58–78 Molesworth Street
☎ 04 474 3000
🕐 Mon–Fri 7:30–4

Colorful, formal flowerbeds in the Botanic Garden

🕂 50B1
National Library
✉ Corner Molesworth and
  Aitken streets
☎ 04 474 3000
🕐 Mon–Fri 9–5, Sat 9–4:30,
  Sun 1–4:30
🍴 Café on premises ($$)
♿ Good
🎟 Free

Archives New Zealand
✉ 10 Mulgrave Street
☎ 04 499 5595
🕐 Mon–Fri 9–5, Sat 9–1
  (exhibitions only)
🎟 Free

🕂 50B1
✉ Mulgrave Street
☎ 04 473 6722
🕐 Daily 10–5. Closed Good
  Fri, 25 Dec
🎟 By donation

🕂 50B1
✉ Pathway leads in from
  Lambton Quay
☎ 04 471 9503 (information
  on guided tours)
🕐 Accessible on tours
♿ Good if accompanied
❓ Not open for unguided
  sightseers
🎟 Free

🕂 50B1
✉ via Ashton Fitchett Drive
☎ 04 381 1200
🕐 Road closes 5PM
  Apr–Sep, 8PM Oct–Mar
♿ Good 🎟 Free
54

NATIONAL LIBRARY AND ARCHIVES NEW ZEALAND

The National Library's modern building contains reference copies of books and periodicals retained throughout New Zealand's history. An important part of the archive is the famous Alexander Turnbull Library of 55,000 historic New Zealand and worldwide publications, bequeathed on Turnbull's death in 1918. Included are a number of rare first editions, including perhaps the world's finest collection of work by John Milton, the English poet.

Close by is Archives New Zealand, where special papers and treasures relevant to New Zealand history are stored and displayed. Included among a number of historical documents is the 1840 Treaty of Waitangi, and a 1776 letter of instructions to Captain James Cook.

OLD ST PAUL'S CHURCH

The old church dating from 1866, so called to distinguish it from the new 1972 cathedral, is now used mainly for concerts rather than prayer. However, its fine colonial Gothic style and its history have secured it as a property of the Historic Places Trust, thus safeguarding its future.

PARLIAMENT BUILDINGS ●●●

The most distinctive of the Parliament Buildings complex in downtown Wellington is the Beehive, designed by Sir Basil Spence and erected in 1982. It houses ministerial offices and the Cabinet Room. Next to it is the Parliament House – New Zealand's one-chamber parliament – and the adjacent building is the Parliamentary Library. Nearby are Government Buildings, the world's second largest wooden building, built in 1876, which now houses the Victoria University of Wellington Law Faculty and the restored early Cabinet Room.

TE PAPA TONGAREWA (▶ 19, TOP TEN)

WELLINGTON WIND TURBINE

This high-tech "windmill" on an exposed site on a Brooklyn hilltop is visible from much of the city. A 225kW Danish turbine harnesses the wind's force. It is part of a larger research project to evaluate wind-generated electricity. The view over Wellington and Cook Strait is a bonus.

What to See Around Wellington

DAYS BAY AND EASTBOURNE ✪

Although these village suburbs, nestling on hilly slopes on the eastern shores of Wellington's harbor, are connected to the city by road and ferry, they feel worlds away. The two beaches are 15 minutes' walk apart. Behind Eastbourne village, with its cafés, craft, and antique shops, the Butterfly Creek track is a favored local walk, while Williams Park, behind Days Bay, is popular for picnics.

✚	50B1
🕐	Up to eight sailings per day
🍴	Blue Penguin café at Days Bay
🚌	81, 83 via Petone
⛴	The Dominion Post Ferry from Queens Wharf

THE DOWSE ✪✪

Situated in Lower Hutt in the Hutt Valley, to the north of Wellington, this is an established local collection of contemporary New Zealand art, glassware, and artefacts from local Maori culture.

From time to time various special local and touring exhibitions are mounted, for which an entry fee is charged.

✚	50B1
✉	35 Laings Road, Lower Hutt
☎	04 570 6500
🕐	Mon–Fri 10–4, Sat–Sun & hols 11–5
🍴	Café on premises
🚌	83 via Petone
🚉	Waterloo Interchange, then buses to Lower Hutt
♿	Free

Left: *Modern Civic Square is the location of Wellington's Information Centre*

FELL ENGINE MUSEUM ✪✪

Beyond the city, the Wairarapa offers a variety of rural attractions. The Fell Engine at Featherston is a special steam locomotive that was used on the railroad over the Rimutaka ranges, before the tunnel was built.

The Rimutaka Incline walkway (☎ 04 564 8551 – DoC Rimutaka Forest Park information center) follows the route of the former line from the edge of the Wellington conurbation. At 18km, the walk takes four to five hours to complete.

✚	50B1
✉	Fell Engine Museum: Corner Lyon & Fitzherbert streets, Featherston
☎	06 308 9379
🕐	Daily 10–4
♿	Good
💷	Donation

Did you know ?

The Chatham Islands, an isolated group of islands 850km east of Wellington, was the first inhabited place to welcome the new millennium. Their local time is just 45 minutes ahead of another close contender, Gisborne, mainland New Zealand's most easterly city, and one of the closest to the International Date Line.

Opposite: *the rich interior of Old St Paul's Church, constructed exclusively with native timber*

+ 50B1

Plimmerton, Paekakariki
or Paraparaumu (☎ 04
498 3000) then buses
71–74

Shopping mall opposite
station at Paraparaumu

**Southward Vintage
Car Museum**

✉ Otaihanga Road,
Waikanae; 55km north of
Wellington

☎ 04 297 1221

🕐 Daily 9–4:30.
Closed Good Fri,
25 Apr, 25 Dec

🚌 Tour buses

♿ Good

💵 Cheap

*A copper car, one
of the more
unusual exhibits
in the Southward
Vintage Car
Museum*

KAPITI COAST

Centred on the dormitory suburbs of Paekakariki and
Paraparaumu to the north of Wellington, the Kapiti Coast is
known for its fine white sandy beaches and good watersports facilities. Kapiti Island, 5km offshore, is a bird
sanctuary with restricted access. Boat trips depart from
Paraparaumu.

Southward Vintage Car Museum, located near
Paraparaumu, boasts one of the largest and most
extensive private collections of vintage automobiles found
anywhere in the world.

+ 50B1

✉ 30km north of Masterton

☎ 06 375 8004

🕐 Daily 9–4/4:30

+ 50B1

♿ Freely accessible

🚌 20; also tour buses

+ 50B1

✉ Wilton Road, Wilton

☎ 04 475 3245

🕐 Daily sunrise–sunset

🚌 14 Wilton 💵 Free

MOUNT BRUCE NATIONAL WILDLIFE CENTRE

An important sanctuary for New Zealand's endangered
species. Look for a kiwi, tuatara or takahe.

MOUNT VICTORIA LOOK-OUT

Rising from Wellington's inner suburbs, this 196m peak
offers a splendid (but usually windy) view of the city and
harbor. It is thought to have been used as a look-out point
by Maori, whose name, Matai-rangi, means "to watch the
sky." Walk or drive to the top.

OTARI–WILTON'S BUSH GARDEN

New Zealand's largest collection of indigenous plants is
cultivated and displayed here in 90ha of parkland and 5ha
of cultivated gardens. Habitats include native bush, natural
forest, an alpine garden, and a fernery. A profusion of
birdlife thrives in the garden.

A Drive Around Wellington

Wellington's Marine Drive commences on Oriental Parade, near the eastern end of Courtenay Place. Note the many narrow and one-way streets in the city center.

Once on Oriental Parade, continue round Oriental Bay past Mount Victoria (➤ 56).

To drive up Mount Victoria, take Majoribanks Street opposite Courtenay Place then follow signs along narrow streets to the Admiral Byrd Memorial and Look-out.

Follow Oriental Parade around Point Jerningham into Evans Bay, passing boating facilities and slipways. Turn left on to Cobham Drive, passing the northern end of the airport runway, then keep left out to the next point.

Shelly Bay Road follows the other side of Evans Bay to Point Halswell. Note the Massey Memorial to former Prime Minister William Ferguson Massey (1856–1925).

The route continues down past Scorching, Karaka and Worser Bays. Continue through Seatoun and the Pass of Branda to rejoin the coast.

Breaker Bay Road follows a bleak stretch of coastline at the harbor entrance. Offshore is Barrett Reef, the craggy rocks where the *Wanganella* ran aground in 1947 and the inter-island ferry *Wahine* foundered in 1968. Moa Point Road leads to the southern end of the airport runway. Continue round Lyall Bay to Island Bay for more views out across Cook Strait.

Return to the city either via Happy Valley and Ohiro and Brooklyn roads to Willis Street and Lambton Quay, or via The Parade and Adelaide Road back to Cambridge Terrace and Courtenay Place.

Distance
40km

Time
2½ hours

Start/end point
Courtenay Place
➕ 50B1

Lunch
Zino's Restaurant ($$)
✉ 351 The Parade, Island Bay
☎ 03 383 8256
🕐 Lunch Sun–Fri, dinner nightly

Wellington's waterfront has been transformed into a place of boardwalks, cafés, restaurants, theaters, and museums.

Typical art deco architecture in Napier

Napier

Hawkes Bay is a picturesque region of hills sweeping down to the central east coast, a fertile plain popularly known as "the fruit bowl of New Zealand." It is also a thriving wine producer, with a number of older vineyards. Tragically, the twin cities of Napier and Hastings suffered an earthquake in 1931.

The rebuilding of Napier in the contemporary architecture of the time has made its fascinating art deco design an attraction and the traffic-free malls in the center of the town create a pleasant shopping environment.

CAPE KIDNAPPERS

The world's largest known mainland colony of Australasian gannets lies 32km southwest of Napier at the southernmost tip of Hawke Bay. These large seabirds arrive in July and lay their eggs in October and November, hatching about six weeks later. The best time to visit the reserve is between October and April.

MARINE PARADE ⭐⭐

Attractions along the esplanade include **Hawkes Bay Museum** which has an interesting audio-visual section devoted to the 1931 earthquake. Other intriguing displays include one devoted to eastern Maori culture and another to art deco from around the world. At **Marineland**, seals, sealions, penguins, and dolphins can all be seen, some in performing shows. Swimming with the dolphins is another option. At the **National Aquarium of New Zealand**, a huge fish tank housing several different species forms the centerpiece where sharks, turtles, crocodiles, plus a number of other animals, are resident. Divers brave enough can even join the inmates of the giant fish tank. If you're a nature-lover, you should visit the kiwi, where you can discover all you want to know about these birds. Here these shy nocturnal birds are kept in natural surroundings and can be seen feeding.

TE MATA PEAK ⭐

A narrow road climbs via Havelock North to the top of this 399m viewpoint offering a spectacular panorama over the Heretaunga Plains.

The peak forms part of the 98ha Te Mata Park, which has good walking routes.

TONGARIRO NATIONAL PARK (► 18, TOP TEN)

New Plymouth

With the development of oil and gas reserves in the region, the city of New Plymouth in northern Taranaki has become the "energy capital." It is equally well known for its parks and gardens, and as the hub of a prosperous dairying region. This in part is due to the fertile deposits from Mount Taranaki, the region's dominant landmark.

MOUNT TARANAKI ✪✪✪

Visible from parts of New Plymouth and most of the Taranaki region, Mount Taranaki, also known as Mount Egmont, rises 2,518m from the coastal plain. This mountain was named by Captain Cook after he first sighted it in 1770. It was named for the Earl of Egmont, who had been First Lord of the Admiralty prior to Cook's departure).

The surrounding 33,000ha Egmont National Park has a small winter ski-field and several walking tracks. The weather conditions can be unpredictable on the mountain, but this does not deter the many climbers attracted by it.

- 50A3
- ✉ North Egmont Visitor Centre, Egmont Road
- ☎ 06 756 0990
- ⏱ Open access
- 🎫 Free

Lush greenery in Pukekura Park

PUKEITI RHODODENDRON TRUST ✪✪

A trust operates these gardens featuring brilliant displays of rhododendrons and azaleas amidst 320ha of native bushland. The best time to visit is September to November, and in late October the city promotes these and other gardens as part of a Rhododendron Week.

- 50A3
- ✉ Carrington Road; 23km from New Plymouth
- ☎ 06 752 4141
- ⏱ Daylight hours daily
- ♿ Few 🎫 Cheap

PUKEKURA PARK ✪

Chief among many parks in the city, these gardens have fountains, a fernery, woodland, and two lakes as features.

Adjoining Pukekura Park, but separated by a concert bowl, is the more formal Brooklands Park where there is a rhododendron dell and European-style flower gardens, as well as sporting grounds.

- 50A3
- ✉ Liardet Street
- ☎ 06 759 6080 (New Plymouth visitor information)
- ⏱ Both gardens free
- ♿ Few

Upper South Island

Despite being one-third larger in area than the North Island, the South Island has only one-quarter of the country's population. The scenery is internationally reknowned for its beauty and variety.

Several national parks lie in the northern half of the South Island, from the bush and beach scenery of Abel Tasman National Park in Nelson province to the great glaciers of Westland on the west coast, a place of legend where men have searched for jade, gold, coal, and timber. In between, the Southern Alps and their foothills offer alpine vistas and a host of opportunities for walking and observing wildlife.

Christchurch is the South Island's international gateway and its largest city. Considered the most "English" of New Zealand's cities, it stands on the edge of the Canterbury Plains.

> *"The great drawback to New Zealand comes from the feeling that after crossing the world and journeying over so many thousand miles, you have not at all succeeded in getting away from England"*

ANTHONY TROLLOPE
Australia and New Zealand
(1873)

Helicopter is the best way to reach Franz Josef glacier

UPPER SOUTH ISLAND

5

4

3

Cape Foulwind
Westpor
Charleston
6

Paparoa
National Park
Punakaiki
**Pancake Rocks
& Blowholes**

Greymouth
Shantytown
7

Lake
Brunner

Hokitika
Lake
Mahinapua
Lake Otira
Kaniere

Ross

Arthur's Pass
2400m
Mt Murchison

2

Harihari

White Heron Sanctuary

WESTLAND

Whataroa
6

2795m
Mt Arrowsmith

CA

Franz Josef
Gillespies Point Franz Josef Glacier Fox
Fox Glacier
Aoraki
Mount Cook
National Park

Arrowsmith Range

Lake
Coleri

Mount Hu

Methve

Westland
National
Park
3498m
Mt Tasman
Mt Cook 3754m
Tasman Glacier
2545m
The Thumbs

Rangitate

Haast
3157m
Mount
Cook

Two Thumb Range

Lake
Tekapo

Rangitata

Plains Village

Jackson Head Jackson
Bay
Cascade Point

Mount Aspiring
National Park
3027m
Mount
Aspiring

Southern Alps

Haast
Pass

Ben Ohau Range

Lake
Pukaki

Mackenzie
Country

Fairlie

Opihi

Canterbury

Temuka
8
Pleasant Poir

1

Lake
McKerrow

Dart

Olivine Range

Young Range

Hunter Range

Lake
Obau

Twizel

Lake
Benmore

Kirkliston Range

The Hunters Hills

Timaru **Caroline
Bay**

Rees

Treble Cone
2088m
6

Lake
Wanaka

Lake
Hawea
8

Omarama

Otematata

Lake
Aviemore

1

Shotover

Clutha

A **Wanaka**

B

Waimate

C

62

Cape Farewell
Farewell Spit
Kahurangi Point
Collingwood
Golden Bay
1213m
Mt Stevens
Takaka
Totaranui
Cape Stephens
D'Urville Island
Kapiti I.
Kahurangi National Park
Motueka
Abel Tasman National Park
Kaiteriteri
Marlborough Sounds
Paraparaumu
Oparara
Karamea
NELSON
Motueka
Motueka
Tasman Bay
Pelorus Sd
Kenepuru Sd
Queen Charlotte Sd
Cook Strait
Porirua
Upper Hutt
Kahurangi National Park
Tasman Mts
Nelson
Richmond
6
Havelock
Picton
Arapawa I.
WELLINGTON
Lower Hutt
Karamea Bight
Motupiko
Brightwater
Richmond Range
Wairau
Renwick
Blenheim
Cloudy Bay
Turakirae Head
Granity
Denniston
1875m
Mt Owen
Rotoroa
St Arnaud
MARLBOROUGH
Seddon
Cape Campbell
Buller Gorge
Murchison
Lake Rotoiti
Waihopai
Avatere
Buller
Lake Rotoroa
Victoria Forest Park
Reefton
Victoria Range
Spenser Mts
Nelson Lakes National Park
Inland Kaikoura Range
1
Clarence
1834m
Mt Ajax
Lewis Pass
Hanmer Forest Park
Hanmer Springs
Seaward Kaikoura Range
Kaikoura
■ Whale Watching Tours
Kaikoura Peninsula
Arthur's Pass National Park
Lake Summer
1612m
Mt Tekoa
Waiau
Hurunui
Cheviot
1987m
Mt Crossley
Culverden
7
Puketeraki Range
Porter Heights
Ashley
Rangiora
Pegasus Bay
Kaiapoi
■ Antarctic Centre
■ Orana Park Wildlife Trust
Darfield
Waimakariri
Christchurch
Heathcote
Air Force Museum
Ferrymead
1 ■ Historic Park
Lyttelton
lains
Rakaia
Lake Ellesmere
Banks Peninsula
Akaroa
Ashburton
inwald
Akaroa Harbour
ERBURY
Canterbury Bight
Canterbury Bight

0   20   40   60   80   100 km

D   E   F

Christchurch

Founded as a Church of England colony in 1850, much of the charm of Christchurch rests with those colonial beginnings, the graceful lines of some of its early Gothic stone buildings contrasting with those of more contemporary design. The city is named after England's Oxford University college, where the city's founding father was educated.

Much of interest lies in the compact downtown area, with the willow-lined Avon River, complete with ducks, ornate bridges, boatsheds, and punts, winding around its cathedral and lively central square. Beyond the city center numerous parks and gardens grace the flat suburbs, giving Christchurch the tag of Garden City. To the southeast, the Port Hills separate the city from its port at Lyttelton on Banks Peninsula and New Zealand's only French settlement, Akaroa.

As the hub of the South Island's air, rail, and road services, the city also makes a good touring base. Many long-distance bus trips start and finish here, with options such as whale-watching at Kaikoura, swimming at Hanmer's hot springs, taking a train through the Alps, skiing in winter, or even visiting Aoraki/Mount Cook, New Zealand's highest mountain, within a day's touring.

Students punting on the river in Christchurch in time-honored tradition

What to See in Christchurch

ARTS CENTRE

Packed with food and craft stands and live entertainment at weekends, this graceful complex, once part of the university, is equally charming on weekdays. Stores, workshops, and galleries sell and display arts and craft works, making it a good place to look for quality souvenir items and gifts at any time, and there are several cafés, restaurants, and bars on the premises. The professional Court Theatre group performs here regularly.

- 66A1
- Worcester Boulevard
- 03 366 0989
- Daily 10–4:30
- Food stands on premises
- Tourist tramway
- Few; assistance suggested
- Free

AVON RIVER

This stream adds a restful charm to the city center as it meanders through Christchurch and there are pleasant walks along its banks. Boats, punts, and canoes can be hired – enquire at the visitor center.

The Town Hall complex overlooking the river includes a concert hall, theater, conference rooms, and restaurant.

- 66A1
- Visitor Centre, Old Chief Post Office, Cathedral Square
- 03 379 9629
- Mon–Fri 8:30–5/6, Sat–Sun 8:30-4:30/5

BOTANIC GARDENS

The 30ha Botanic Gardens lie within Hagley Park, a vast sports and recreation area on the fringe of the central business district. Set amid the wooded lawns are a number of themed gardens (rose, rock, azalea), and there are many displays of flowering trees and exotic plants.

The glasshouses feature numerous displays of orchids, ferns, and tropical plants, among others.

- 66A1
- Rolleston Avenue
- 03 941 6841
- Gardens: daily 7AM–1 hour before sunset; conservatories: 10:15–4
- Restaurant & café
- Christchurch tramway
- Few

CANTERBURY MUSEUM

This is a general collection relating to New Zealand history and ethnology. Two specialist exhibits are of particular interest: The Moa Hunters, featuring life-size dioramas of early Maori and the giant flightless bird (long extinct), and the excellent Hall of Antarctic Discovery, with relics from the Scott expedition and others. The museum has a gift store and organizes four free guided tours daily.

- 66A1
- Rolleston Avenue
- 03 366 5000
- Daily 9–5 (later in summer)
- Coffee shop at museum
- Tourist tramway
- Good
- By donation

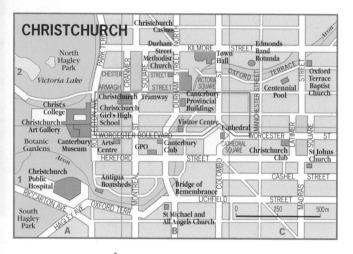

CHRISTCHURCH

66B2

Cnr Durham/Armagh streets

Mon–Sat 10:30–3; Oct–May Sun 2–4

CANTERBURY PROVINCIAL BUILDINGS ✪

Built in 1858 beside the Avon River, this neo-Gothic-style complex reflects the city's English heritage and the early days when New Zealand had 13 independent provinces.

Christchurch Casino on Victoria Street

66A1

Montreal Street/Worcester Boulevard

03 941 7300

Daily 10–5 (Wed until 9)

Café, wine bar

Tourist tramway

Good Free

CHRISTCHURCH ART GALLERY ✪

Located at the corner of Montreal Street and Worcester Boulevard, the gallery exhibits New Zealand and British paintings, as well as a whole range of other works of art, including ceramics and photography.

CHRISTCHURCH CATHEDRAL ✪✪

The building of this Gothic-style edifice, crowned with a 65m copper-clad spire, was begun in 1864 at the heart of the original Church of England settlement. The cathedral was completed 40 years later. There are 133 steep stone steps up to the top of the bell tower and, as might be expected, the views from the top are worth the effort.

CHRISTCHURCH TRAMWAY ✪✪

Electric trams first came to Christchurch in 1905 but the network was closed down in the early 1950s. Now, restored vintage trams take tourists on a newly created scenic route through the city, taking in many of the best sites and shopping areas. Full-day passes are available and passengers can hop on and off to suit.

Did you know ?

One of the enduring sights in Cathedral Square is a figure dressed in black robes and a wizard's hat who makes it his business to mock both the preachers and the visitors who gather round. The wizard holds forth at about 1PM on most days.

SCIENCE ALIVE! ✪✪

Located in the old Christchurch railroad station, this thoroughly modern interactive science facility offers an educational yet fun-filled experience for people of all ages.

✚ 66B1
✉ Cathedral Square
☎ 03 366 0046
🕐 Opens 8:30AM; tower closed till 11:30AM Sun
🚊 Christchurch Tramway
♿ Good ⬛ By donation

✚ 66B2
✉ From Cathedral Square
☎ 03 366 7830
🕐 Summer daily 9–4; winter 9–6
♿ Difficult access
⬛ Cheap

Above: *the Christchurch Tramway is a good way of seeing the city's sights*

✚ 63D2
✉ 392 Moorhouse Avenue
🕐 Mon–Fri 9–5; Sat–Sun 10–6

Boat trips around the bays of Banks Peninsula leave from Akaroa Harbour

What to See Around Christchurch

AIR FORCE MUSEUM ☺
The Royal New Zealand Air Force Museum, at the former air base at Wigram in Christchurch's western suburbs, reflects the history of military aviation in New Zealand from the earliest days. As well as the aircraft and related displays, authenticated with figures and scenery, there are several hands-on exhibits.

63D2
⊠ Main South Road, Wigram
☎ 03 343 9532
🕐 Daily 10–5. Closed 25 Dec
🍴 Café on premises
🚌 8, 25   ♿ Good
💲 Cheap

AKAROA AND BANKS PENINSULA ☺☺
Within days of the British declaring sovereignty over New Zealand in 1840, a shipload of French settlers founded Akaroa on Banks Peninsula to the southeast of Christchurch, and it has remained French in spirit.

Mountainous Banks Peninsula is a large volcanic outcrop, with the original craters now forming Lyttelton and Akaroa harbors (➤ 70, 71). Allow time for a cruise.

63E2
⊠ SH75; 83km from Christchurch
☎ 03 379 9629 (Christchurch visitor center)
🍴 Several restaurants, especially French
🚌 Day tours available

CHRISTCHURCH GONDOLA ☺☺
Ride up the side of Mount Cavendish by aerial cable-way from the terminal near the Lyttelton tunnel entrance at Heathcote for a great view over Christchurch and Lyttelton. There are a restaurant, a kiosk, a store and a Time Tunnel display (admission extra) at the upper terminal.

63D2
⊠ Bridle Path Road
☎ 03 384 0700
🕐 Daily 10–evening
🍴 Restaurant   🚌 28
♿ None   💲 Moderate

FERRYMEAD HISTORIC PARK ☺☺
This is a living museum of transport and technology with a working tramway, railroad and village, plus displays about household appliances, wirelesses, fire engines, and aviation, among others. Hundreds of mechanical musical instruments are another feature. Several volunteer groups are responsible for different portions of the park.

63D2
⊠ 269 Bridle Path Road, Heathcote
☎ 03 384 1970
🕐 Daily 10–4:30. Closed 25 Dec
🚌 30   ♿ Good
💲 Cheap

HANMER SPRINGS ☺☺
Formerly an alpine spa, this outdoor recreation center 135km north of Christchurch offers skiing in winter and adventure options such as jet-boat rides and bungy jumping. The prime attraction, however, is the Thermal Reserve with its hot pools set in landscaped grounds.

63D3
⊠ Pools: Amuri Road
☎ 03 315 7128
🕐 Daily 10–4. Closed 25 Dec
🍴 Café   ♿ Good   💲 Cheap

A Walk Around Christchurch

Start at the visitor information center in Cathedral Square, pausing to take a look at the cathedral (➤ 67).

Stroll due west along Worcester Street to the Avon River (➤ 65). The Bridge of Remembrance to the left was built to commemorate Kiwi troops who died during World War I.

Worcester Street continues as a renovated boulevard. After crossing Montreal Street opposite the new Christchurch Art Gallery (➤ 67), pause at the Arts Centre (➤ 65). At weekends, when there are outdoor stalls as well as the many shops, allow extra time. Next the Canterbury Museum (➤ 65) looms in front.

Continue for two blocks north on Rolleston Avenue, passing Christ's College, and turn east into Armagh Street. Pass Cranmer Square.

At the Durham Street intersection, note the grand architecture of the Canterbury Provincial Buildings (➤ 66).

Cross the Avon again to enter Victoria Square. Across the square, past statues and fountains, note the award-winning (1972) architecture of the Town Hall.

Turn right from Armagh into quaint Spanish-style New Regent Street, then back to Cathedral Square where there is usually interesting activity including street performers. The Southern Encounter Aquarium is also located here. Much of this route follows the Christchurch Tramway (➤ 67); if in doubt, follow the tracks or take a ride.

There is always something to watch in Cathedral Square

Distance
2.5km

Time
1½ hours plus stops

Start/end point
Cathedral Square
✚ 66B1

Lunch
Annie's Wine Bar and Restaurant ($$)
✉ Arts Centre, 2 Worcester Boulevard
☎ 03 365 0566

Hands-on at the Centre

INTERNATIONAL ANTARCTIC CENTRE ✪✪✪

Located next to the airport, and the Operation Deep Freeze base of the United States Air Force, the center displays both the geography and science of the southern polar regions with exhibits and wide-screen movies. Some of the highlights include a walk-through ice cave and an Antarctic aquarium. There is also a souvenir shop and an interactive room.

✚ 63D2
⊠ Orchard Road, Harewood
☎ 03 353 7798
🕐 Daily 9–5:30 (8:30PM summer). Closed 25 Dec
🍴 Café 🚌 Airport bus
♿ Good 💰 Cheap

LYTTELTON ✪✪

Canterbury's picturesque port, the largest in the South Island, is reached by road tunnel or over the Port Hills by car. Take a harbor cruise, walk around the steep, historic streets to the Timeball Station – a castellated structure that was used to signal the ships in the harbor by dropping a ball each day – or visit the Lyttelton Museum, which has maritime and colonial displays, and an Antarctic gallery.

✚ 63D2
⊠ SH74; 13km from Christchurch
☎ 03 379 9629 (Christchurch visitor information)
🕐 Launch to Diamond Harbour about hourly
🚌 28

ORANA PARK WILDLIFE TRUST ✪

Animals from New Zealand, Africa, Australia, Asia, and the Americas can be seen in this 80ha wildlife park, New Zealand's largest, which specializes in breeding rare and endangered species. In addition to this, there is a farmyard featuring domestic animals, a reptile house, native bird aviaries, and a nocturnal kiwi house, plus lots more.

✚ 63D2
⊠ McLeans Island Road, Harewood
☎ 03 359 7109
🕐 Daily 10–4:30. Closed 25 Dec
🍴 Restaurant
📞 Phone details
♿ Few 💰 Cheap

THE TRANZALPINE (► 24, TOP TEN)

A Drive to Akaroa and Banks Peninsula

From Christchurch, the route heads southeast to Banks Peninsula; there are alternatives for the return.

From Cathedral Square, drive south along Colombo Street. After several blocks, turn west (to the right) on to Moorhouse Avenue and follow signs to the left for Akaroa, leading to SH75.

The route leaving the city leads across flat country to Birdlings Flat, skirting Lake Ellesmere, a shallow wetland separated from the sea by the gravelly Kaitorete Spit.

Turn inland to Little River, a former railway terminus.

From here the road climbs steeply up to Hilltop for views over Akaroa Harbour, the crater of an extinct volcano.

The road then drops steeply and follows the harbor round to Akaroa (➤ 68), 83km from Christchurch.

Akaroa's Gallic ancestry is clearly visible in street names and architecture. In addition to local walks, gardens, a museum, and a historic lighthouse, a worthwhile attraction is a cruise around the harbor. The *Canterbury Cat* operates daily at 1:30PM for two hours, often sighting Hector's dolphins, penguins, and seals.

There are alternative return routes to Christchurch, including the high, narrow Summit Road. Either follow the ridge around to Hilltop, or cross over to follow a hilly route round to Lyttelton Harbour. From there, choose the tunnel, the Dyers Pass route to Christchurch, or take the Evans Pass route on to Sumner Beach, and then continue your journey to Christchurch.

Distance
166km

Time
Allow a full day

Start/end point
Cathedral Square
➕ 66B1

Lunch
L'Hotel Wine Bar & Café ($$)
✉ 75 Beach Road, Akaroa
☎ 03 304 7559

View across Akaroa Harbour, one of the most attractive areas of Banks Peninsula

71

What to See in the Upper South Island

ABEL TASMAN NATIONAL PARK (▶ 21, TOP TEN)

AORAKI/MOUNT COOK NATIONAL PARK (▶ 25, TOP TEN)

FOX AND FRANZ JOSEF GLACIERS ✪✪✪

These two huge glaciers, some 25km apart, are the main features of Westland National Park. Both are unique in that they descend as low as 300m in temperate zones.

Guided tours and hikes, including helicopter trips, are available from the villages of Fox and Franz Josef, where there are visitor centers. The headquarters of the national park, which includes a display about the glaciers, is at Franz Josef.

✚ 62B2
⊠ Glaciers: SH6; 187km from Greymouth

Franz Josef Visitor Information
☎ 03 752 0796
① Summer daily 8:30–6; winter 8:30–12, 1–5

HAAST ✪✪

Situated 117km south of Fox Glacier (▶ above), this tiny settlement marks the entrance to the Haast Pass route through the Southern Alps to Wanaka and Queenstown.

Now designated a World Heritage Area by Unesco, the Haast region includes New Zealand's most extensive area of wetlands, rainforests, coastal lagoons and swamps. Displays at the visitor center relate to the abundant wildlife of the area and its early inhabitants.

✚ 62A1
⊠ SH6; 345km southwest of Greymouth
☎ 03 750 0809 (Haast visitor information)
① Daily 8:30–4
🚌 Daily from the glaciers and Queenstown

KAHURANGI NATIONAL PARK ✪✪

Formerly called Northwest Nelson Forest Park, this is the second largest national park in New Zealand. Largely mountainous with very few roads through it, the park is known for the Heaphy Track, a 77km walking route. Forest and bush-clad countryside covers the marble and limestone karst country, which is riddled with extensive cave systems, most of which are closed to the public.

✚ 63D5
⊠ Via SH60 to Collingwood; 136km from Nelson
☎ 03 528 1810
① Open access to park
🚌 Shuttle transfers arranged locally
🅿 Free access

KAIKOURA ✪✪

This small town on the rocky Kaikoura Coast was formerly a whaling station and has become popular as a whale-watching center with trips available year round. The main road north and south of the town offers splendid coastal scenery, and the local Maori Leap Cave (3km south) is famous for its limestone formations.

✚ 63E3
⊠ SH1; 191km north of Christchurch
☎ 03 319 5641 (Kaikoura visitor information)
🚌 Dailky from Christchurch, Blenheim, Picton
🚆 TranzCoastal daily from Christchurch, Blenheim, Picton

LAKE TEKAPO   ✪✪

Accessible from the main road between Christchurch and Mount Cook village, the lake lies at the northern end of the barren Mackenzie Country basin. Glacial deposits account for the amazing turquoise color of the water.

A picturesque small stone chapel situated on the edge of the lake, built to commemorate the pioneer farmers of the area, is a favourite tourist stop. Alpine flights are also available from here.

✚ 62C2
✉ SH8; 226km west of Christchurch
🍽 Restaurants available
🚌 Daily from Christchurch and Queenstown

MARLBOROUGH VINEYARDS   ✪✪✪

The Marlborough district is New Zealand's sunniest region, and as a result the countryside around the town of Blenheim is the country's premier wine-making region. Marlborough sauvignon blanc is especially renowned and wine-tasting tours are available. Several vineyards have café-style restaurants, where you can dine outdoors in summer.

Brayshaw Historic Museum Park includes displays of old farming equipment, there is a mock colonial village to explore along with several attractions to keep the children amused.

✚ 63E4

Brayshaw Historic Museum Park
✉ New Renwick Road
☎ 03 578 1712
🕐 Mon–Sat 10–4; Sun 1:30–4
💷 Cheap

Whale-watching off the Kaikoura Coast

NELSM

⊕ 63E4
✉ SH6; 438km north of Christchurch
☎ 03 548 2304 (Nelson Visitor Information Centre)

Suter Art Gallery
✉ Bridge Street
☎ 03 548 4699
🕐 10:30–4:30

NELSON ⊕⊕

Sheltered by hills, the sunny city of Nelson is the center of a rich horticultural, forestry, and fishing region. It is also noted for its arts and crafts, especially pottery, which is displayed at local galleries. Foremost is the **Suter Art Gallery**. The Wearable Art Awards held annually in September at the World of Wearable Art showcase weird and wacky fashions made from unlikely materials.

Paths in the Botanical Reserve lead up to a viewpoint known as the Centre of New Zealand. There is excellent swimming at Tahuna Beach and in the nearby Maitai, Aniseed, and Lee rivers.

⊕ 63D3
✉ Via SH6 & SH63; 119km south of Nelson
☎ 03 521 1806
🕐 Free access to park
🚌 Daily bus from Nelson

NELSON LAKES NATIONAL PARK ⊕

Inland, south of Nelson, the tiny village of St Arnaud is the main gateway to this mountainous park best known for its twin lakes of Rotoroa and Rotoiti. St Arnaud stands on the shores of the latter and is popular for boating, fishing, and hiking.

⊕ 63E4/F5
✉ SH1; 28km north of Blenheim
☎ 03 573 7477 (Picton visitor information)
⛴ From Wellington
🍴 Portage Hotel on luncheon cruise (10:15–4:30)

At the entrance to the Marlborough Sounds

PICTON AND THE MARLBOROUGH SOUNDS ⊕⊕⊕

Picton, at the head of Queen Charlotte Sound, is the commercial center for the sea inlets formed from the drowned valleys known as the Marlborough Sounds. It is also the South Island port for the inter-island ferry service from Wellington.

In a covered dry dock is the hulk of the 1853 clipper ship *Edwin Fox* – a former carrier of tea, troops, convicts, meat, and coal; it is currently being restored. Picton Museum has an interesting local collection, including whaling relics.

Launch cruises and fishing trips can be taken around the Sounds and there are also walking tracks, some requiring several days to complete. There are lodge accommodations on some of the walks, e.g. the Queen Charlotte Track.

Lake Pukaki, with Aoraki/Mount Cook in the background

Did you know ?

The last stronghold of the kaki or black stilt, the world's rarest wading bird, is among the rivers threading through the Mackenzie Basin. Once common in New Zealand, numbers have dwindled to fewer than 100 due to loss of their breeding habitat. A captive breeding program has been established at the Black Stilt Aviary just outside the town of Twizel.

TWIZEL AND LAKE PUKAKI ★★

The road from Twizel to Mount Cook village (➤ 25) runs alongside the glacier-fed Lake Pukaki, known for its distinctive blue coloring. At 16sq km, it is the South Island's fifth largest lake.

Originally built as a servicing town for the giant Upper Waitaki hydro-electricity scheme, Twizel has survived to service the tourist industry and local rural scene.

✚ 62B1
⊠ SH8; 284km southwest of Christchurch
☎ 03 435 0802 (Twizel Field and information center)
🍴 Cafés and hotel restaurant
🚌 Daily from Christchurch and Queenstown

WESTLAND NATIONAL PARK (➤ 72, FOX AND FRANZ JOSEF GLACIERS)

WHITE HERON SANCTUARY ★

Amid the lagoons that lie on the northern fringes of Westland National Park, beside the Waitangi-roto River, lies New Zealand's only breeding site for the white heron. These majestic birds nest between November and February, during which time tours may be taken to see them. Tours leave from Whataroa, and include a jet-boat ride, a ride in a minivan, and a short walk.

✚ 62B2
⊠ SH6; 154km south of Greymouth
☎ 03 753 4120
🕐 Access controlled
🚌 Daily from Greymouth, Nelson, and the glaciers
♿ Not good 💲 Expensive

75

Food & Drink

New Zealanders like to eat and drink well and visitors will find no shortage of good places to eat. As well as authentic New Zealand food, often served in restaurants displaying a "Taste New Zealand" sign, there are many ethnic restaurants to choose from, and a profusion of new cafés offering lighter foods in casual settings at lower prices.

Above: *informality is the keynote of New Zealand restaurants*
Above right: *opening up a Maori hangi* (➤ 95)

The international fast-food chains are well represented and takeaway (food-to-go) places are common. Many shopping malls have a food court offering a selection of inexpensive light meals.

Meat

Lamb is the traditional meat of New Zealand, usually served roasted with mint sauce or jelly, but beef, pork, and chicken are all popular. Canterbury lamb is esteemed. Hogget is one-year-old (the tenderest) lamb.

Meat pies, filled with steak, mince or chicken, sometimes with cheese or potato toppings, are a New Zealand favourite.

Seafood

Seafood delicacies are available throughout the country either as starters or main courses. These include Nelson scallops, Marlborough and Coromandel mussels, Bluff (deep sea) oysters from the far south of the South Island, and West Coast whitebait. Seafood soups, especially chowders, are also popular.

Fish dishes feature snapper, orange roughy, hapuka (groper), flounder, blue cod, and John Dory. Salmon are reared in the south but trout, although a popular game-fish, is not caught commercially, nor offered in restaurants.

Fruit and Vegetables

A wide variety of locally grown vegetables is available, from supermarkets or direct from the growers in the countryside, where prices are generally less expensive and the produce is freshest. *Kumara* is a native sweet potato. Seasonal fresh fruit, grown locally, includes apples, peaches, pears, plums, and apricots.

The prickly skinned kiwifruit (bright green inside) was known as Chinese gooseberry until the Kiwis decided to market them as their own. Now they are branded as Zespri.

Desserts

Fresh strawberries, raspberries, and boysenberries are a summer favorite, served with creamy New Zealand ice cream, and in places you can "pick your own" fruit straight from the vine. The dessert New Zealanders claim as their own (although Australians disagree with this) is pavlova, a meringue base covered with a layer of whipped cream and topped with fresh fruit.

Kiwi fruit, just one of the many fruits that thrive in New Zealand's fertile soil and temperate climate

Drink

New Zealand's tap water is safe to drink, although bottled water is popular. Water from streams and lakes should be purified before drinking. A pot of tea is an essential part of Kiwi hospitality, while good coffee is widely available in cafés. Fresh milk and fruit juice are inexpensive.

Traditionally, New Zealanders are a nation of beer drinkers and, while brands like DB, Lion, and Steinlager dominate, many local boutique brewery labels have added interest to the market. New Zealand wines are now well established internationally, with Marlborough sauvignon blancs acclaimed. Leading labels include Cloudy Bay and Montana.

Mealtimes

Kiwis usually have a light breakfast and lunch, and a substantial evening meal ("dinner" or "tea"), eaten between 6PM and 8PM. Most motels offer cooking facilities, but will provide a cooked breakfast on request.

Lower South Island

Fiordland, one of the world's largest and most spectacular national parks, covers the southwest corner of the South Island, its shoreline slashed by great inlets stretching far inland into a region of forests and lakes. Gateway to the area is the resort of Te Anau, situated on the shore of its great lake.

Lovers of the great outdoors are attracted to photogenic Queenstown, on Lake Wakatipu. Within easy reach of fiords, skiing, and various adventure options, it is a world famous holiday destination. South is Invercargill, regional center of Southland and the main departure point for New Zealand's often forgotten third island, Stewart Island, well off the main tourist track and a haven for bush wildlife.

Dunedin, sometimes dubbed "the Edinburgh of the South," is an important city for commerce and university education.

"The danger is that,
when people find out
what an interesting place
New Zealand is, they may
come in crowds.
…I strongly advise you
not to make too much of
the tourist sights except
for yourselves "
GEORGE BERNARD SHAW
What I Said in New Zealand (1934)
published in the *Auckland Star* (1934)

Queenstown
The South Island's second largest lake, Wakatipu, with the Remarkables mountain range as a backdrop, provides a dramatic and picturesque setting for Queenstown, nestled snugly on its northeastern shore.

This is undoubtedly New Zealand's premier resort for adventure and action, offering a host of exhilarating activities ranging from jet-boating on the nearby Shotover and Kawarau rivers to helicopter trips over the mountains, from bungy-jumping to skiing at Coronet Peak, from parachute jumps to white-water rafting.

Less sensational but equally appealing are the gentler pursuits of lake cruising on an old steamboat, walking, backpacking, and fishing. For those who prefer just to look, there are museums, parks, and gardens around the town. Not to be missed is the Skyline Gondola (➤ 23) for spectacular views of the lake.

The nightlife here is just as lively, with many bars, cafés, and restaurants to choose from and a range of entertainment lasting long into the night. Shoppers and strollers are well catered to, with the traffic-free streets of The Mall and Church Street running down to the waterfront, the colorful focal point of the town.

Formerly a gold-mining town, Queenstown has come to rely on tourism since the beginning of this century and now makes every possible effort to attract visitors from around the world.

Queenstown, on Lake Wakatipu, reinvented itself as an adventure capital, offering commercialized bungy-jumping, jetboat, and white-water rafting thrills

The TSS Earnslaw steamer making a visit to Walter Peak Farm across the lake

What to See in Queenstown

TSS *EARNSLAW*

The lake steamer TSS *Earnslaw*, built in 1912, operates frequent cruises from its wharf near downtown. This "lady of the lake" offers local sightseeing trips and excursions to Walter Peak Farm, a high-country sheep station across the lake where sheep-shearing and dog-handling are demonstrated.

🕂 82C4
✉ Steamer Wharf
☎ 03 442 7500
🕓 Departs regularly
🍴 Evening cruise offers dinner at Walter Peak
♿ Few 💲 Expensive

KIWI AND BIRDLIFE PARK

A number of avaries, including some housing endangered species, a native bush area, and a nocturnal kiwi house are the main attractions here. Ponds and landscaping provide an attractive, natural setting.

🕂 82C4
✉ Brecon Street
☎ 03 442 8059
🕓 Daily 9–5
💲 Moderate

QUEENSTOWN GARDENS

Queenstown Gardens, with trees and shrubs, flower gardens, and recreational areas, cover a small promontory jutting into the lake. They were established in 1867. There are views through the trees of the mountains, from the short walk along the beach from downtown.

Williams Cottage, at the entrance to the Gardens, is one of Queenstown's oldest buildings.

🕂 82C4
✉ Marine Parade or Park Street
☎ 03 442 4100 (Queenstown visitor information)
🕓 Unrestricted access
♿ Few

QUEENSTOWN MOTOR MUSEUM ✪

A collection of vintage cars, motorcycles, and aircraft, plus an assortment of motoring memorabilia, make up this museum next to the Skyline Gondola terminal. Special exhibitions change on a regular basis.

🕂 82C4
✉ Brecon Street
☎ 03 442 8775
🕓 Daily 9–5:30

SKYLINE GONDOLA (➤ 23, TOP TEN)

UNDERWATER WORLD AQUARIUM ✪

An underground observatory with huge windows, situated at the end of the main pier on Queenstown Wharf, allows spectators to view at close quarters the lake's wildlife, such as trout and eels.

🕂 82C4
✉ Rees Street
☎ 03 442 8437 🕓 9–5:30
♿ None 💲 Cheap

A Walk Around Queenstown

The first part of this stroll around Queenstown is flat, but the second part involves a climb in the countryside.

From the wharf at the foot of The Mall, outside Eichardt's Hotel, walk towards the peninsula jutting out into the lake. This short stroll, either along the lake's beach or adjacent footpath, leads to the Queenstown Gardens (➤ 80).

Here paths lead through flowers and trees, as well as past recreational amenities such as tennis courts and a bowling rink. There are views back through the trees to downtown Queenstown or out over the lake. The southeastward view across the lake incorporates the Remarkables range.

Loop around to the access road (Park Street) and walk up the streets behind Queenstown. Turn left at the top of Sydney Street into Hallenstein Street, then right into Edgar and Kent streets.

From here note the signposted Queenstown Hill Walkway. Follow this path for some 4.5km, rising to a height of about 850m. The path alternates through bush (mostly exotic trees, including pine and fir), with the vegetation becoming scrubbier at higher altitudes. There are patches of schist rock and a small tarn on the way.

The view opens out over the town, the lake and surrounding mountains to reveal the steep glaciated valleys and mountainsides of the district.

Return by the same route.

The Botanical Gardens in Queenstown, occupying a small promontory jutting into the lake

Distance
10km

Time
3.5 hours

Start/end point
Foot of The Mall
✚ 82C4

Lunch
A drink and "counter lunch" at Eichardt's Hotel ($)
✉ The Mall, Queenstown
☎ 03 442 8369

LOWER SOUTH ISLAND

Jackson Head

Jackson Bay

Cascade Point

Mount Aspir

National P

Awarua Point

Tasman Sea

Big Bay

Martins Bay

Lake McKerrow

Olivine Range

Dart

Yates Point

3027m

Mount Aspiring

Milford Sound

Darran

Rees

Holyford

Richardson Mts

Shotover

208

Bligh Sound

1692m

Milford Sound

Mitre Peak

Homer Tunnel

Kinloch

Greenstone

2819m

Glenorchy

Coronet Peak

George Sound

Franklin Mts

Milford Track

Skippers Canyon

Arr to

Caswell Sound

Charles Sound

Stuart Mts

Glade House

Skippers Canyon

Queenstown

Fran

Thomson Sound

Murchison Mts

Skyline Gondola

Secretary Island

Te Anau Caves

Lake Te Anau

Livingston Mts

6

Doubtful Sound

Fiordland National Park

Kepler Mts

Te Anau

Eglinton Valley

Lake Wakatipu

Kingston

Dagg Sound

West Arm

Mararoa

Ayre Mts

Wilmot Pass

Kepler Track

Lake Manapouri

Breaksea Sound

West Arm Underground Powerhouse

Hunter Mts

Manapouri

Takitimu Mts

Mossburn

Lumsden

Resolution Island

L. Monowai

SOUTHLAND

Dusky Sound

Cameron Mts

Kaiherekoau Mts

Waiau

Riversdale

West Cape

Chalky Inlet

Lake Hauroko

Lake Poteriteri

Aparima

Oreti

Winton

Go

Mataur

Puysegur Point

Otautau

Te Waewae Bay

Tuatapere

6

Pahia Point

Riverton

1

Mataura

Solander Island

Centre Island

Invercargill

Bluff

Stirling Point

Bluff Harbour

Toetoes Bay

Waip

Poi

Foveaux

Codfish Island

980m

Mount Anglem

Mason Bay

Halfmoon Bay (Oban)

Ruapuke Island

Peterson Inlet

Strai

750m

Mt Allen

1

Stewart Island

South West Cape

A   B   C

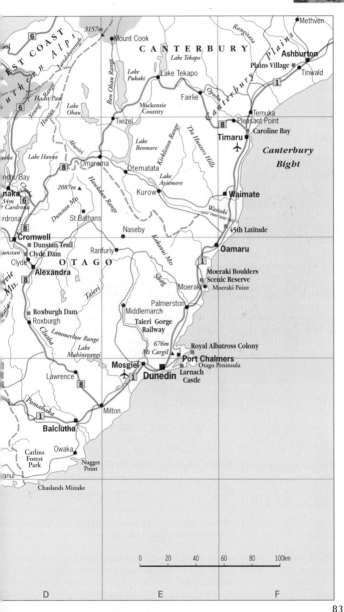

WEST COAST

Southern Alps

3157m

Mount Cook

CANTERBURY

Lake Tekapo

Methven

Ashburton

Plains Village

Tinwald

Lindisbrough

Haast Pass

Young Range

Hunter

Lake Ohau

Ben Ohau Range

Lake Pukaki

Lake Tekapo

Fairlie

Mackenzie Country

Rangitata

Canterbury Plains

1

Temuka

8   Pleasant Point

Caroline Bay

Timaru

Lake Hawea

Twizel

Lake Benmore

Kirkliston Range

The Hunters Hills

Canterbury Bight

8

Omarama

Ahuriri

Otematata

Lake Aviemore

ndhu Bay

naka

34m
Cardrona

rdrona

2087m

Dunstan Mts

Hawkdun Range

Kurow

Waimate

Waitaki

6

Clutha

St Bathans

Naseby

45th Latitude

Oamaru

Cromwell

Dunstan Trail

Clyde Dam

Clyde

OTAGO

Ranfurly

Kakanui Mts

1

Moeraki Boulders

Scenic Reserve

Moeraki   Moeraki Point

8

Alexandra

Taieri

Sbag

Roxburgh Dam

Roxburgh

Lammerlaw Range

Middlemarch

Palmerston

rvie
Mts.

Clutha

Lake
Mahinerangi

676m
Mt Cargil

Taieri Gorge
Railway

Royal Albatross Colony

Port Chalmers

Mosgiel

Otago Peninsula

8

Lawrence

1

Dunedin

Larnach
Castle

Pomahaka

Milton

Balclutha

Catlins
Forest
Park

Owaka

Nugget
Point

anui

Chaslands Mistake

0   20   40   60   80   100km

D   E   F

83

What to see Around Queenstown

ARROWTOWN ✪✪

📍 82C4
✉ 20km from Queenstown
☎ 03 442 4100 (visitor information)
🍴 Restaurants & cafés
🚌 Local shuttle service

Old-fashioned Arrowtown

With its stone cottages and non-native trees such as sycamore and oak, this charming old gold-mining town is less commercialized than Queenstown. The main shopping street is delightful to stroll along, and a visit to the Lakes District Centennial Museum is worthwhile.

The return trip to Queenstown via Lake Hayes is especially beautiful in the autumn.

CORONET PEAK ✪✪

📍 82C4
✉ 15km from Queenstown
☎ 03 442 4620 (Coronet Peak visitor information)
🍴 Winter only
🚌 Shuttle in ski season

Between June and October this is one of the region's leading ski-fields, but it is worth visiting at any time of the year as the 15km drive offers sky-high views over Lake Wakatipu and the surrounding countryside. During the season a regular bus service operates to the field.

SKIPPERS CANYON ✪✪

📍 82C4
✉ 28km from Queenstown
☎ 03 442 4100 (Queenstown visitor information)
🕐 Half-day tours depart 8:45AM and 2PM
🚌 Small tour buses
💷 Expensive

The narrow cliff-side road leading to the remnants of Skippers, a former gold-mining township, is the main attraction here, but only experienced drivers should attempt it (rental vehicles are excluded).

One of the Queenstown sites known for bungy-jumping is near the road's end, at the bridge spanning the narrow gorge over the Shotover River upstream. The Shotover Jet speed-boat thrill rides are in a gorge on the lower section of the river.

A Drive from Queenstown to Milford Sound

Whether by rental car or coach tour, the most popular excursion from Queenstown is the round trip to Milford Sound (► 16). Allowing time for a cruise on the fiord, it is a 12-hour day.

From Queenstown drive 6km round to Frankton on SH6A to join SH6, southbound.

The road winds around the bluffs above Lake Wakatipu, passing Kingston at its southern end before rising over a crest to enter farmland.

The main road leads to Lumsden to pick up SH94 west, but follow the signposted short cut via Five Rivers.

From Mossburn, the road crosses progressively more barren countryside. Note a loop road to Manapouri before arriving at Te Anau (► 90).

From Te Anau, SH94 turns northwards, then runs parallel with Lake Te Anau and enters the beech forest of the Eglinton Valley. As the mountains close in, the Divide is crossed into the upper Hollyford Valley and the road climbs up to the Homer Tunnel. On emerging, the road zig-zags down to Milford Sound where a hotel, an air-strip, and other facilities have been built. The road ends here and return is via the same route, although tours offer coach/fly options.

A cruise on the fiord, with its high steep sides and waterfalls, is recommended. The facilities at Milford are limited, but basic accommodations and catering are available.

In winter (June – August) the road is prone to snow and there is a risk of avalanches.

Distance
291km each way

Time
A 12-hour day with stops

Start/end point
Downtown Queenstown
✚ 82C4

Lunch
Meals available on Milford Sound cruise boats

Cruise ships are dwarfed by the grandeur of Milford Sound

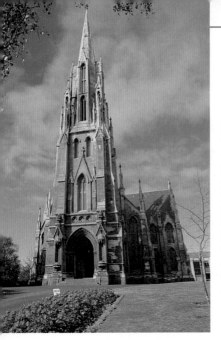

Dunedin

The town was founded in 1848 by settlers of the Free Church of Scotland at the head of Otago Harbour, a long waterway sheltered by the scenic Otago Peninusla (➤ 89). Prosperity soon followed in the wake of the 1860s Otago goldrush, and the city became New Zealand's wealthiest, leaving a legacy of handsome, well-preserved buildings. Above all though, Dunedin is known

Dunedin's first church, a Presbyterian Gothic-style church built between 1868 and 1873

as a university city (New Zealand's first university was founded here in 1869), with a lively social, arts, and music scene.

The Octagon, at the center of the town, is dominated by a statue to the Scottish poet Robbie Burns and the imposing Anglican St Paul's Cathedral. The fact that the country's only whisky distillery is located in Dunedin is another reminder of its Scottish connections.

Extensive formal gardens (the first to be created in New Zealand) at the northern end of the city include a rose walk, the Ellen Terry garden, a rhododendron dell (best seen between October and November when the shrubs are in bloom), azalea beds, and winter gardens.

HOCKEN LIBRARY

Part of the university, the library (founded by Dr T.M. Hocken, 1836–1910) houses a collection of historic books, early manuscripts, paintings, and photographs relating to Otago, New Zealand, and the Pacific. General browsing of shelves is not permitted.

OLVESTON

This handsome stone Jacobean-style house, built at the beginning of the 20th century, illustrates the lifestyle of its wealthy owners, the Theomin family. Most of the well-preserved contents of the house, including a collection of paintings, were collected during the family's extensive travels overseas.

➕ 83E2
✉ 90 Anzac Avenue
☎ 03 479 8868
🕐 Mon–Fri 9:30–5, also Tue 6–9; Sat 9–noon
♿ Good
💷 No Charge

➕ 83E2
✉ 42 Royal Terrace
☎ 03 477 3320
🕐 Set tours daily: 9:30, 10:45, noon, 1:30, 2:45 and 4
♿ None 💷 Moderate

Multicolored portal outside the Otago Settlers Museum

OTAGO MUSEUM ✪✪
Noted for its Maori and Pacific Island sections, the museum, founded in 1868, also features a good natural history section, a maritime exhibition, and several decorative arts items from Asia. The Discovery World section, with many scientific hands-on exhibits, brings the museum up to date.

* 83E2
* 419 Great King Street
* 03 474 7474
* Daily 10–5
* Few; assistance required
* Free

OTAGO SETTLERS MUSEUM ✪✪
This fine museum tells the story of Otago's history and includes interesting sections on early Maori habitation and Chinese settlement during the gold rush era. There is a photographic gallery featuring early settler portraits, manuscripts, and displays of their relics. Also housed here are two steam locomotives.

* 83E2
* 31 Queens Gardens
* 03 477 5052
* Daily 10–5. Closed Good Fri, 25 Dec
* Assistance suggested
* Cheap

SIGNAL HILL ✪✪
Located in suburban Opoho, this 393m peak offers a fine view over central Dunedin. A viewing terrace erected in 1940 marks the centenary of the British pioneers in New Zealand.

* 83E2
* End of Signal Hill Road
* 03 474 3300 (Dunedin visitor information)
* Unrestricted
* Few

TAIERI GORGE RAILWAY ✪✪
The four-hour return trip along the craggy Taieri Gorge aboard a diesel-hauled excursion train leaves Dunedin station every afternoon. In addition to the scenery, there are many Victorian bridges and viaducts to admire.

Dunedin railroad station, a grand Edwardian building with an ornate interior, is a city landmark.

* 83E2
* Dunedin railroad station
* 03 477 4449
* Departs 12:30 winter; 2:30 summer
* Refreshments on train
* Few   Expensive

What to See in the Lower South Island

BLUFF

Invercargill's port of Bluff, 27km south of the city, lies below Bluff Hill at the tip of the South Island. A road leads up to a look-out with views across the harbor to Stewart Island (▶ 90). Highway One goes to land's end at Stirling Point, with its much-photographed signpost indicating distances to Cape Reinga, London, and elsewhere.

82C2
SH1; 27km south of Invercargill
03 214 6243 (Invercargill visitor information)

CATLINS

This coastal strip at the southeast corner of the South Island has a spectacular coastline of rugged, lonely beaches, while inland lie tracts of undisturbed forests where there is a wealth of flora and fauna.

83D2
138km east of Invercargill
03 415 8371 information

CROMWELL

Located east of Queenstown, in the barren landscape of Central Otago, Cromwell was partly rebuilt in the 1980s when the Clutha River was dammed to form Lake Dunstan. The story of the Clyde Dam, and Cromwell's origins as a gold-mining settlement, is presented in the town's information center and museum.

83D3
SH6 and SH8; 57km from Wanaka
03 445 0212 (Cromwell visitor information)
Scheduled coach service daily from Christchurch, Queenstown & Dunedin

FIORDLAND NATIONAL PARK (▶ 16, TOP TEN)

INVERCARGILL

New Zealand's southernmost city, Invercargill lies in a flat pastoral region close to Foveaux Strait. Its main attraction is the **Southland Museum and Art Gallery** in Queens Park, a complex featuring displays about natural history, colonial settlers, and the Maori heritage. Two important attractions are an enclosure displaying New Zealand's rare lizard-like tuatara reptile and a presentation about the wildlife of the sub-Antarctic islands – five uninhabited rocky clusters lying up to 700km to the south.

82C2

Southland Museum and Art Gallery
Gala Street, Queens Park
03 218 9753
Mon–Fri 9–5, Sat–Sun 10–5
Good
Free or donation

LAKE MANAPOURI AND DOUBTFUL SOUND

The best way to enjoy the beauty of this large lake is by taking a cruise. The most popular trip is to West Arm where an underground hydro-electric power scheme has been built. Access to the powerhouse is by coach along a 2km tunnel. Some tours continue across the Wilmot Pass to the remote sea inlet of Doubtful Sound, where another cruise can be taken.

82B3/A3
12km south of Te Anau
03 249 6602
Cruises depart 9:30 summer, 9:45 winter for sound; also 1:30 summer for West Arm only
Not good
Expensive

MILFORD SOUND (▶ 16, TOP TEN)

MILFORD TRACK ✪✪

Often described as "the finest walk in the world," this four-day hike runs from the top of Lake Te Anau to Milford Sound. Boat access is required at both ends, and walkers can choose either to travel independently, overnighting in park huts, or join a fully guided trip. Both options require advance bookings.

🞢 82B4
☎ 03 249 8514 for bookings
Ⓤ Expensive

OTAGO PENINSULA ✪✪

The craggy peninsula guarding Dunedin's harbor is renowned for its wildlife, but also has a number of man-made attractions. Among these is Larnach Castle, built in 1871, complete with ballroom and battlement. Following a checkered history, the castle has been renovated and is open to view. There are limited accommodations. Glenfalloch Gardens are also popular.

There are several wildlife reserves on the peninsula, but the most special is the **Royal Albatross Centre** at Taiaroa Head, the world's only mainland colony for giant royal albatrosses. The colony has a special viewing gallery and there is an interesting visitor center.

🞢 83E2

Royal Albatross Centre
✉ Harrington Point Road
☎ 03 478 0499 (booking essential)
🕙 10AM–dusk (from 9AM in summer). Closed 25 Dec
🍴 Cafeteria at Center
♿ Visitor center good; viewing observatory not good
Ⓤ Moderate
❓ Viewing observatory closed mid-Sep to mid-Nov

The royal albatross, ungainly and awkward on land but a superb flier; it sometimes stays in the air for days on end

Did you know ?

The eggs laid by the giant royal albatross in November hatch roughly 11 weeks later, with each parent taking turns to incubate them. The chicks remain at Taiaroa until the following September when they take their first flight. Adult birds range over 2,000km of sea, returning to breed in alternate years. They have wingspans of up to 3m.

✚ 82C1	
☎ 03 219 0009 (Stewart Island visitor information)	
📷 Foveaux Express catamaran (☎ 03 212 7660)	
✈ Southern Air (☎ 03 218 9129)	

STEWART ISLAND AND RAKIURA NATIONAL PARK ★★

New Zealand's third island, covering 1,746sq km, lies 27km south of the South Island. It can be reached either by air from Invercargill or by catamaran from Bluff. This rugged island is known primarily for fishing, bush-walks and birdlife. Although there are few roads on the island, there are good walking tracks, including the arduous 10-day North-West Circuit. The island's only town, Halfmoon Bay, offers a selection of accommodations.

✚ 82B3
Cruise and Cave
✉ Te Anau lakefront wharf
☎ 03 249 7416 (Real Journeys)
🕐 Depart 2PM and 8:15PM (6:45PM in winter)
♿ Not suitable
✋ Moderate

TE ANAU ★★

Gateway to Fiordland National Park (➤ 16), the township beside Lake Te Anau is the main center for the district and the starting point for a number of walking tracks and boat cruises. One of the latter takes visitors across the lake to the **Te Anau Glowworm Caves**, where there is a glow-worm grotto, the insects' sticky threads lighting the roof of a cave like twinkling stars. In Te Anau, as well as the National Park Visitor Centre, where there is historical and practical information about all aspects of the park, the Wildlife Centre is of interest. Here the takahe (*Notornis mantelli*), a flightless bird once thought to be extinct, is exhibited.

✚ 83D4
☎ Wanaka visitor information: 03 443 1233; Mount Aspiring National Park Centre: 03 443 7660
✋ Free access to park

WANAKA ★★

The eastern gateway of the Haast Pass to South Westland, Wanaka stands on the shores of Lake Wanaka. Although lacking the pizazz of its neighbor Queenstown, it nonetheless has just as much to offer in outdoor thrills, with skiing in season at Treble Cone, Cardrona, and Waiorau skifields. It is the headquarters of Mount Aspiring National Park.

For an enjoyable day's adventure, walk to the Rob Roy Glacier from West Matukituki Valley (3–4 hours return). But be warned: Alpine weather is unpredictable and blizzards can occur suddenly at any time of year. Take warm, all-weather clothing, food, map and compass, and ideally, a local guide.

Above: *a number of trips and outdoor activities in Fiordland start from Lake Te Anau*

Where To...

Above: *Maori warrior*
Right: *Art deco architecture in Napier*

Upper North Island

Prices

Prices, inclusive of goods and services tax (► 104), are approximate. They are based on a three-course meal for one without drinks and service:

$ = under $25
$$ = $25–50
$$$ = over $50

Auckland

Antoine's Restaurant ($$$)

Renowned upmarket New Zealand food cooked in modern French manner.

✉ 333 Parnell Road ☎ 09 379 8756 ⏰ Lunch Mon–Fri, also dinner and supper Mon–Sat. Closed Sun

Cin Cin on Quay ($$$)

Popular café in downtown Ferry Building.

✉ 99 Quay Street ☎ 09 307 6966 ⏰ Mon–Fri from 11AM, Sat–Sun from 9:30AM

Iguaçu ($$)

Popular, informal brasserie in Parnell.

✉ 269 Parnell Road ☎ 09 358 4804 ⏰ Lunch and dinner daily; also brunch Sat and Sun

Kelly's Café ($)

Light meals at the harbor edge, adjacent to the Kelly Tarlton Underwater World attraction.

✉ 23 Tamaki Drive, Orakei ☎ 09 528 5267 ⏰ Daily 8–5 🚌 Any 72- to 76-

New Orient ($$)

Chinese restaurant in city center.

✉ Strand Arcade, 233 Queen Street ☎ 09 379 7793 ⏰ Lunch and dinner daily

one red dog ($)

Busy pizza cafés in two trendy suburbs.

✉ 151 Ponsonby Road, 156 Hurstmere Road ☎ 09 360 1068, 09 488 0077 ⏰ Lunch to late

Pearl Garden Restaurant ($)

Sizzling Cantonese food with large menu.

✉ 1 Teed Street, Newmarket ☎ 09 523 3696 ⏰ Daily noon–2:30, 5-9PM

Sails Restaurant ($$$)

Popular restaurant with views of harbor bridge.

✉ Westhaven Marina; 2km from downtown ☎ 09 378 9890 ⏰ Lunch and dinner daily

Saints Waterfront Brasserie ($$)

Suburban restaurant with harbor views.

✉ 425 Tamaki Drive, St Heliers ☎ 575 9969 ⏰ Lunch and dinner daily, also brunch Sat and Sun from 10AM

Sake Bar Rikka ($$)

Japanese food as it ought to be.

✉ 208 Victoria Street West ☎ 09 377 8239 ⏰ Lunch and dinner daily

The Loaded Hog ($)

Lively tavern serving light meals. Their own beers are brewed on the premises.

⏰ 204 Quay Street ☎ 09 366 6491 ⏰ Daily 11–10

Tony's Restaurant ($$)

Good value menu, featuring New Zealand fare.

✉ 32 Lorne Street ☎ 09 373 2138 ⏰ Lunch Mon–Fri, dinner daily

Toso ($)

Excellent Japanese food in cosy surroundings.

✉ 474 Queen Street ☎ 09 357 0866 ⏰ Mon–Fri 11:30-2:30, 5:30-10:00, Sat and Sun 5:00-11:00

Wings ($$)

Restaurant and bar over-looking popular suburban beach.

✉ 71 Tamaki Drive, Mission Bay ☎ 09 528 5419 ⏰ Lunch and dinner daily; open 11:30AM weekdays, 10:30AM Sat and Sun

Bay of Islands

Copthorne Hotel & Resort Bay of Islands ($$)
Quality eating in a pleasant location.
- ✉ Tau Henare Drive, Waitangi
- ☎ 09 402 7411
- ⏱ Dinner daily; snacks at other times

Ferryman's Restaurant ($$)
Seafood in a nautical location; 5km from Paihia.
- ✉ 3 Beechy Street, Opua wharf
- ☎ 09 402 7515 ⏱ Daily 10AM–10PM

The Gables Restaurant ($$)
Seafood and other meals in a vintage building.
- ✉ The Strand, Russell ☎ 09 403 7618 ⏱ Dinner daily in summer; Jun–Sep, Wed–Sun

Tides Restaurant ($$)
Seafood specialties in an interesting setting.
- ✉ Williams Road, Paihia
- ☎ 09 402 7557
- ⏱ Dinner daily in summer, Mon–Sat in winter

Rotorua

Aorangi Peak ($$$)
A "Taste New Zealand" winner with mountain-top views.
- ✉ Mountain Road, Mount Ngongotaha, on Rotorua's outskirts ☎ 07 347 0046
- ⏱ Lunch and dinner daily

Chapmans Restaurant ($$)
Excellent New Zealand buffet.
- ✉ Centre Hotel, Froude Street, Whakarewarewa ☎ 07 348 1189 ⏱ Lunch and dinner daily

Lewisham's ($$)
European-style cuisine in Rotorua's main street.
- ✉ 1099 Tutanekai Street
- ☎ 07 348 1786

- ⏱ Lunch Mon–Fri, daily dinner. Closed Tue dinner

Orchid Garden Café ($$)
Light meals, including breakfast, amid flowers and gardens.
- ✉ 1220 Hinemaru Street
- ☎ 07 347 6699 ⏱ Daily

Street Café ($$)
Light trendy cuisine; outdoor option at Prince's Gate Hotel.
- ✉ 1057 Arawa Street
- ☎ 07 348 1179 ⏱ Lunch and dinner daily

Valentine's ($$)
All-you-can-eat family dining with a huge menu.
- ✉ Corner Fenton & Amohau streets ☎ 07 349 4490
- ⏱ Lunch and dinner daily

Zanelli's ($$)
Italian cuisine
- ✉ 1243 Amohia Street
- ☎ 07 348 4908

Taupo

Edgewater Restaurant ($$$)
Restaurant overlooks the lake at the Copthorne Hotel Manuels, 2km from the town center. Imaginative New Zealand dishes.
- ✉ Lake Terrace, Taupo
- ☎ 07 378 5110 ⏱ Dinner only

Finn MacCuhal's Irish Pub ($$)
Guinness and good food.
- ✉ Corner Tongariro & Tuwharetoa streets, Taupo
- ☎ 07 378 6165
- ⏱ Lunch and dinner daily

Nonni's ($$)
Popular café and restaurant in central Taupo.
- ✉ 3 Tongariro Street ☎ 07 378 6894 ⏱ Daily 7AM–late

Licensing Laws
A licensed restaurant is able to sell wine, beer or spirits with a meal. A BYO (bring your own) license means that customers can take in their own wine, although they may be charged for corkage, including use of glasses: Some places are both licensed and BYO. Wine bars and licensed cafés are becoming more common throughout the country.

Lower North Island

Alcohol and the Law
The legal drinking age for imbibing in bars and taverns is 19. Bars are open daily, all day, until 11PM or later. Remember that roadside tests for alcohol and blood samples may be taken at random from any driver of a vehicle.

Wellington

Back Bencher Pub & Cafe ($$)
Light meals with pub atmosphere.
✉ 34 Molesworth Street
☎ 04 472 3065 🕓 Lunch and dinner daily

Bengal Tiger ($$)
Popular Indian restaurant with good-value evening buffet.
✉ 98 Victoria Street ☎ 04 472 8706 🕓 Lunch Mon–Fri, dinner daily

Boulcott Street Bistro ($)
Light and interesting bistro food in lively surroundings.
✉ 99 Boulcott Street
☎ 04 499 4199 🕓 Lunch Mon–Fri, dinner Mon–Sat

Chameleon ($$$)
Top hotel dining at the InterContinental Hotel.
✉ Grey Street ☎ 04 495 7851 🕓 Lunch Mon–Fri, dinner Mon–Sat

Chocolate Fish Café ($$)
Seaside café favoured by the *Lord of the Rings* stars (► 47).
✉ 497a Karaka Bay Road, Scorching Bay ☎ 04 388 2808 🕓 Lunch daily

Cobb & Co Restaurant ($)
Family dining in suburban Hutt Valley.
✉ The Esplanade, Petone, ☎ 04 939 2622 🕓 Daily 10:30–10

Fujiyama Japanese ($$$)
Good Japanese hot-plate-style restaurant.
✉ 36 Taranaki Street
☎ 04 801 8699 🕓 Lunch and dinner daily

The Grill ($$$)
Eat posh cuisine at the Duxton Hotel.
✉ 148 Wakefield Street
☎ 04 471 5711 🕓 Dinner daily

Il Casino ($$)
Top Italian-style food in downtown area.
✉ 108 Tory Street ☎ 04 385 7496 🕓 Lunch and dinner daily

Kirkcaldie & Stains ($)
"The Birdcage" restaurant in Wellington's leading department store.
✉ 165–177 Lambton Quay
☎ 04 472 5899 🕓 Mon–Fri 9:30–4:30, Sat 10–3

The Lido ($$)
For a good breakfast and lunch, try this busy café, across from the information center.
✉ Corner Victoria & Wakefield streets ☎ 04 499 6666 🕓 Mon–Sat

Logan Brown ($$$)
Dining in style in a former bank.
✉ Corner Cuba & Vivian streets ☎ 04 801 5114 🕓 Lunch and dinner daily

The Oriental Thai ($$)
Large Thai menu and friendly service.
✉ 58 Cambridge Terrace
☎ 04 801 8080 🕓 Daily

Short Black Café ($$)
Light meals at the National Library of New Zealand.
✉ 58–78 Molesworth Street
☎ 04 474 3000 🕓 Mon–Fri 9:30–4

The White House ($$$)
Fine dining with harbor views; mainly New Zealand cuisine.
✉ 232 Oriental Parade
☎ 04 385 8555 🕓 Lunch Mon–Fri, dinner daily

Napier

Alfresco's Café ($$)
Delicious Pacific Rim and Mediterranean food.
✉ 65 Emerson Road, Napier
☎ 06 835 1181 🕐 Daily 9:00AM–2:00AM

Bangkok House ($$)
Reasonably priced, authentic Thai cuisine.
✉ 205 Dickens Street, Napier
☎ 06 835 5335 🕐 Lunch and dinner daily

Bayswater ($$)
Small award-winning restaurant with a view over the beach.
✉ Hardinge Road, Ahuriri
☎ 06 835 8517 🕐 Lunch and dinner daily

East Pier ($$)
Popular new brasserie at Port Ahuriri.
✉ Hardinge Road, Ahuriri
☎ 06 834 0035 🕐 Lunch and dinner daily

Peak House ($$)
Restaurant and bar located on the slopes of Te Mata Peak.
✉ Te Mata Peak Road, Havelock North ☎ 06 877 8663
🕐 Lunch Wed–Mon, dinner Wed–Sun

Pierre Sur le Quay ($$)
French Provincial-style award-winner, 2km from city center.
✉ 62 West Quay, Ahuriri
☎ 06 834 0189
🕐 Dinner Tue–Sat, brunch and lunch Wed–Sun

Shed 2 ($$)
Good Hawkes Bay fare served in a pleasant setting.
✉ Corner West Quay & Lever streets ☎ 06 835 2202
🕐 Lunch and dinner daily

New Plymouth

André L'Escargot ($$)
Award-winning French provincial restaurant.
✉ 37 Brougham Street
☎ 06 758 4812 🕐 Mon–Sat 11AM–late

Asian Wok Café ($)
Good value Chinese and Thai selection.
✉ Corner St Aubyn & Dawson streets ☎ 06 758 1828
🕐 Lunch and dinner daily

Chinos Café ($$)
Meat, seafood, pasta and vegetarian.
✉ 117 Devon Street East
☎ 06 758 6843 🕐 Breakfast, lunch and dinner daily

Gables ($$)
Country cooking on the edge of town, with a coffee shop and smorgasbord.
✉ Corner Waihi Road & Fantham Street, Hawera ☎ 06 278 8153 🕐 Mon–Fri 9:30–4, also dinner Wed–Sun

Gareth's ($$)
Elegant spot with a long-standing reputation for freshly prepared, imaginative dishes, fine wines and good service.
✉ 182 Devon Street ☎ 06 758 5104 🕐 Lunch Mon–Fri, dinner daily

Juliana's ($$)
Fine dining and service at the Auto Lodge Motor Inn.
✉ 393 Devon Street ☎ 06 758 8044 🕐 Dinner Mon–Sat

Marbles Buffet ($$)
Roman-themed smorgasbord with meat, vegetarian and oriental dishes in Devon Hotel.
✉ 390 Devon Street East
☎ 06 759 9099 🕐 Dinner daily

A *Hangi*
A Maori *hangi* is a method of cooking on heated stones in an earth oven. Traditionally, the food is sandwiched between leaves, sprinkled with water, and then steamed. Some resort hotels and tour operators offer this option, usually in conjunction with a Maori song and dance performance. At some places the food may be precooked before being finished off *hangi*-style.

Upper South Island

Wineries

Grapes are grown in west Auckland, the Waikato district north of Hamilton, around Gisborne and Napier, at Martinborough near Wellington, in Nelson, in Canterbury, and central Otago. The premier wine-producing district, however, is regarded as the region around Blenheim in Marlborough. Wine Trail brochures are provided by the local tourist offices in these regions, giving the locations and opening hours of the vineyards.

Christchurch

Annie's Wine Bar and Restaurant ($$)
Classic surroundings.
✉ Arts Centre, 2 Worcester Boulevard ☎ 03 365 0566
🕐 Lunch Mon–Sun 11:30–3, dinner daily 5:30–11

Brogues Restaurant ($$$)
Brasserie at Rydges Hotel, in the city center.
✉ Oxford Terrace ☎ 03 379 4700 🕐 Dinner Mon–Sat

Camelot ($$$)
A medieval castle-style dining room offering fine food and service.
✉ 189 Deans Avenue ☎ 03 348 8999 🕐 Dinner daily

Canterbury Tales ($$$)
Award-winning restaurant of the Crowne Plaza Hotel, with a medieval theme, offering dishes prepared from the freshest Canterbury produce, and an extensive wine list.
✉ Corner Kilmore & Durham streets ☎ 03 365 7799
🕐 Lunch Mon–Fri, dinner Mon–Sat

Christchurch Gondola Restaurant ($$$)
Dining with fantastic views – at a price – atop the gondola cable-way.
✉ Mount Cavendish Gondola, 10 Bridle Path Road, Heathcote ☎ 03 384 0707 🕐 Lunch and dinner daily

Dux de Lux ($$)
Very popular establishment with self-service vegetarian restaurant, Tapas Seafood Bar and Tavern Bar serving beers brewed on the premises.
✉ Hereford & Montreal streets ☎ 03 366 6919 🕐 Lunch and dinner daily

French Farm Winery ($$)
Award-winning restaurant in winery on Banks Peninsula.
✉ French Farm, Valley Road, Akaroa ☎ 03 304 5784
🕐 Daily 10–5

Il Felice ($$)
Italian food and decor in downtown Christchurch.
✉ 56 Lichfield Street ☎ 03 366 7535 🕐 Dinner Mon–Sat

Palazzo del Marinaio ($$)
Seafood and other dishes in the city center.
✉ The Shades, 108 Hereford Street ☎ 03 365 4640
🕐 Lunch Mon–Fri, dinner daily

Retour ($$)
Neat dining in a converted band rotunda next to the Avon River. New Zealand specialties complemented by home-made desserts.
✉ 230 Cambridge Terrace ☎ 03 365 2888 🕐 Tue–Sat dinner in winter, daily summer

Sign of the Takahe ($$$)
Elegant dining 6km out of Christchurch in a mock baronial castle. Seafood a specialty.
✉ Dyers Pass Road, Cashmere Hills ☎ 03 332 4052 🕐 Lunch daily, dinner Mon–Sat

Strawberry Fare ($$)
Mouthwatering desserts are the specialty of this down-town restaurant. As well as desserts, savory meals are served throughout the day.
✉ 114 Peterborough Street ☎ 03 365 4897 🕐 Daily

The Tap Room ($$)
Light meals throughout the day and evening.
✉ 124 Oxford Terrace ☎ 03 365 0547 🕐 Lunch and dinner daily

Blenheim

Allan Scott's Winery ($$)
Fresh salads and fine wine in patio setting.
- ✉ Jacksons Road
- ☎ 03 572 9054
- 🕐 Lunch and dinner daily

D'Urville ($$)
Local reputation for good food.
- ✉ 52 Queen Street, Blenheim
- ☎ 03 577 9945
- 🕐 Lunch Mon–Fri, dinner daily

Hunter's Vintner's ($$)
Marlborough's food and wine served in an award-winning vineyard, 8km from Blenheim.
- ✉ Hunter's Vineyard, Rapaura Road
- ☎ 03 572 8803
- 🕐 Lunch and dinner daily

Seymours ($$)
Nice offerings of some of Marlborough's gourmet foods at the Blenheim Country Hotel. Wine list has over 70 wines produced in the area.
- ✉ Corner Henry & Alfred streets
- ☎ 03 578 5079
- 🕐 Lunch and dinner daily

Kaikoura

Caves Restaurant ($$)
Good value restaurant serving snacks and local seafoods.
- ✉ Main Highway South
- ☎ 03 319 5023
- 🕐 Daily from 7AM

Mount Cook

Panorama Room ($$$)
Main dining room of The Hermitage Hotel, with alpine views.
- ✉ Mount Cook Village
- ☎ 03 435 1809
- 🕐 Dinner daily

Nelson

Appelman's Restaurant ($$)
A Lamb Award winner also serving Nelson seafood, pasta, omelets, and salads.
- ✉ 294 Queen Street, Richmond
- ☎ 03 544 0610
- 🕐 Dinner daily

Broccoli Row ($$)
Quality seafood and vegetarian restaurant.
- ✉ 5 Buxton Square, Nelson
- ☎ 03 548 9621
- 🕐 Lunch and dinner Mon–Sat

Ribbetts ($$)
More Nelson seafood and produce, 3km out in Tahunanui suburb.
- ✉ 20 Tahunahui Drive
- ☎ 03 548 6911
- 🕐 Dinner daily

Quayside ($$)
Family restaurant for Nelson seafood and general cuisine.
- ✉ Wakefield Quay
- ☎ 03 548 3319
- 🕐 Continuous from 11:30AM, Sun from 9AM

Picton

Le Café ($)
Modern café on the waterfront.
- ✉ London Quay
- ☎ 03 573 5588
- 🕐 Lunch and dinner daily in summer, Mon–Fri winter

Portage Hotel ($$)
Take a cruise from Picton to this beachfront restaurant for lunch with a view.
- ✉ Linkwater–Kenepuru Road, or 10:15AM Beachcomber cruise from Picton
- ☎ 03 573 4309
- 🕐 Hotel serves three meals daily; cruise lunch only

Westland

Blue Ice Café ($$)
Good, varied international fare amid glacier country. Delicious desserts and good espresso coffee. Jazz music.
- ✉ SH6, Franz Josef Glacier Village
- ☎ 03 752 0707
- 🕐 Lunch and dinner daily

Wild Foods Festival
Held at Hokitika in early March, this festival is an annual extravaganza of gourmet bush-tucker, based on the West Coast's natural food sources. The emphasis is on novel, tasty, and healthy dishes using natural, wild food. As well as the food and drink, entertainment takes place all afternoon.

Lower South Island

Wine and Food Festivals

The annual BMW Wine Marlborough Festival, centered on Blenheim in the second or third weekend of February, is the leading event of its kind in the country. This event showcases the region's reds, whites, and sparkling wines, as well as local gourmet foods. Hot fun under a blazing sun, with live music, and a real party atmosphere.Similar festivals celebrating the pleasures of eating and drinking are held in Hawkes Bay, Christchurch, Martinborough near Wellington, and Auckland's suburb of Devonport.

Queenstown

Avanti ($$)
Italian and local foods in the center of town. Relaxed atmosphere and good service.
☒ **20 The Mall** ☎ **03 442 8503**
🕐 **Lunch and dinner daily**

Bentley's Brasserie ($$$)
First-rate food and views at the Parkroyal Queenstown Hotel.
☒ **Beach Street** ☎ **03 442 7800** 🕐 **10AM–10PM daily**

Berkel's ($–$$)
Renowned for its burgers – huge choice of fillings. Extensive list of beers and wines.
☒ **19 Shotover Street**
☎ **03 442 6950** 🕐 **Daily**

Eichardts Hotel ($)
High-class meals in the mall.
☒ **The Mall** ☎ **03 441 0450**
🕐 **Lunch and dinner daily**

Gantley's ($$)
Reputation for good food and service in an out-of-town renovated ruin.
☒ **Arthurs Point Road** ☎ **03 442 8999** 🕐 **Dinner daily**

Gibbston Valley Vineyard ($$)
Pleasant dining 11km out of town at one of the world's southernmost vineyards.
☒ **Main Highway 6, Queenstown** ☎ **03 442 6910**
🕐 **Lunch daily**

Minami Jujisei ($$)
Reputedly the world's southernmost Japanese restaurant, with a large variety of Japanese dishes. Sushi bar, traditional Tatami room, and Western-style dining room.
☒ **45 Beach Street** ☎ **03 442 9854** 🕐 **Lunch Mon–Fri, dinner daily**

Nugget Point Retreat ($$$)
New Zealand fine food served well at this hotel overlooking the Shotover River gorge, 6km out of Queenstown.
☒ **Arthurs Point Road**
☎ **03 442 7273** 🕐 **Dinner daily**

Promenade ($$)
Good dining near the town center. Excellent service and dishes, many featuring New Zealand lamb.
☒ **Gardens Parkroyal, Marine Parade** ☎ **03 442 7750**
🕐 **Three meals daily**

Reflections ($$)
Excellent value fixed-price Sunday buffet.
☒ **Novotel Queenstown Hotel, Salisbury Road, Fernhill**
☎ **03 442 6600** 🕐 **Dinner daily**

Skyline Restaurant ($$)
Ride the cable gondola for great views and good food, then relax in the lounge with a sundowner cocktail.
☒ **Take gondola in Brecon Street** ☎ **03 442 7860**
🕐 **Dinner daily**

The Cow ($)
Unlikely name for a very popular pizza café. Roaring fire on chilly evenings. Book in advance or expect to wait.
☒ **Cow Lane** ☎ **03 442 8588**
🕐 **Dinner daily**

The Stables ($$)
Fine dining in converted stables at historic Arrowtown, 20km from Queenstown.
☒ **28 Buckingham Street, Arrowtown** ☎ **03 442 1818**
🕐 **Dinner daily**

Dunedin

The Atrium ($$$)
French cuisine in a pleasant setting at Cargills Hotel.
✉ 678 George Street
☎ 03 477 7983 🕐 Lunch and dinner daily

Bell Pepper Blues ($$)
Award-winner with good food, American-style.
✉ 474 Princes Street ☎ 03 474 0973 🕐 Lunch Wed–Fri, dinner Mon–Sat

Portraits Restaurant ($$)
Award-winning fare at the Abbey Lodge Hotel, 2km from city center.
✉ 900 Cumberland Street
☎ 03 477 5380 🕐 Lunch Mon–Fri, dinner daily

Ports of Call ($$)
Hotel dining room in downtown.
✉ Southern Cross Hotel, 118 High Street ☎ 03 474 6003 🕐 Dinner daily

Villa at Ninety Five ($$)
Modern menu, local foods.
✉ 95 Filleul Street ☎ 03 471 9265 🕐 Dinner daily, brunch Sunday

Terrace Café ($$)
New Zealand, Mediterranean, and vegetarian dishes.
✉ 118 Moray Place ☎ 03 47 40686 🕐 Dinner Tue–Sat

Invercargill

Birchwoods Brasserie ($$)
Carvery and à la carte dining at Ascot Park Hotel.
✉ Corner Tay Street & Racecourse Road ☎ 03 217 6195 🕐 Usual hotel meal hours with extended evening times

Donovan ($$)
Fine foods in an old homestead.
✉ 220 Bainfield Road ☎ 03 215 8156 🕐 Dinner Tue–Sun

Drunken Sailor Restaurant ($$)
Choice of snacks or meals at this southernmost point.
✉ Stirling Point, Bluff
☎ 03 212 8855

Te Anau

Baileys ($$)
Café serving sandwiches to seafood.
✉ Main Street ☎ 03 249 7526 🕐 Lunch through dinner; reduced hours in winter

La Toscana ($$)
Tuscan cooking in central Te Anau.
✉ 108 Town Centre ☎ 03 249 7756 🕐 Dinner Mon–Sat

Mackinnon Room ($$)
Elegant dining at the Holiday Inn.
✉ Lake Front Drive ☎ 03 249 7411 🕐 Dinner daily

Wanaka

Amigos ($$)
Casual coffee or dinner from Mexico.
✉ 34a Ardmore Street ☎ 03 443 7872 🕐 Tue–Sun from 6PM

Cardrona Hotel ($)
Bistro by day, restaurant at night, in historic goldfields pub built in 1860s.
✉ Crown Range Road, Cardrona Valley (29km from Wanaka) ☎ 03 443 8153 🕐 Lunch daily, dinner Wed–Sun

Relishes Café ($)
International and New Zealand fare.
✉ 99 Ardmore Street ☎ 03 443 9018 🕐 Daily 9–3, then 6:30–late. Closed Tue in winter

Cobb & Co
This was the name of the first South Island horse and coach company, providing transport around the island on a number of set routes before the days of the railroad and automobile. Their name is remembered in a chain of restaurants.

Tipping and Tax
As a rule, tipping for any sort of service is not a common practice in New Zealand and is not expected. However, if the service has been exceptional, a tip will not be refused.

Always check the menu to see whether the GST tax (► 104) is included or is additional to the prices quoted.

Upper North Island

Prices

Prices are for a double room, excluding breakfast and GST (➤ 104).

$ = single or double rooms at less than $50
$$ = $50–150
$$$ = over $150, including GST

Auckland

Alpers Lodge ($$)
Handy to Newmarket and freeways.
✉ 16 Alpers Avenue,
☎ 09 523 3367

Barrycourt ($$)
Many rooms with kitchens.
✉ 10–20 Gladstone Road,
Parnell ☎ 09 303 3789

Centra Auckland Airport ($$$)
International standard, 4km from airport.
✉ Corner Kirkbride & Ascot Road, Mangere ☎ 09 275 1059
🚌 Transfer from airport on request

Crowne Plaza ($$$)
Located in the center of the business and shopping area.
✉ 128 Albert Street
☎ 09 302 1111

Remuera Motor Lodge & Caravan Park ($)
Budget accommodations and motor camp, 9km from city.
✉ 16 Minto Road, Remuera
☎ 09 524 5126

Sedgwick Kent Lodge ($$$)
Luxury suburban bed and breakfast homestead.
✉ 65 Lucerne Road, Remuera
☎ 09 524 5219

Sky City Hotel ($$$)
Hotel, conference center and casino, adjacent to the Sky Tower in central Auckland.
✉ Corner Victoria & Federal Streets ☎ 09 363 6000

Stamford Plaza Auckland ($$$)
Considered Auckland's top hotel, central city location.
✉ Albert Street
☎ 09 309 8888

Bay of Islands

Copthorne Hotel & Resort Waitangi ($$$)
Coastal location with recreational areas.
✉ Tau Henare Drive, Waitangi
☎ 09 402 7411

Quality Hotel Autolodge ($$)
Central location with 72 rooms.
✉ 8 Marsden Road, Paihia
☎ 09 402 7416

Rotorua

Aywon Motel ($$)
Motel with full kitchens, opposite the Grand Tiara.
✉ 18–20 Trigg Avenue
☎ 07 347 7659

Regal Geyserland Hotel ($$)
Scenic views of Whakarewarewa thermal area.
✉ Fenton Street ☎ 07 348 2039

Royal Lakeside Novotel ($$$)
International hotel adjacent to lake.
✉ 9–11 Tutanekai Street
☎ 07 346 3888

Taupo

Oasis Beach Resort ($$)
Lakeside motor inn, 3km from central Taupo.
✉ 241 Lake Terrace
☎ 07 378 9339

Tui Oaks Motor Inn ($$)
Lakeside location.
✉ 88 Lake Terrace
☎ 07 378 8305

Wairakei Resort ($$$)
Upmarket hotel in Thermal Valley. Golf, tennis, spa.
✉ State Highway 1, Wairakei
☎ 07 374 8021

Lower North Island

Wellington

Brentwood Hotel ($$)
Located just four minutes from Wellington airport, 120 rooms.
✉ **16 Kemp Street**
☎ **04 387 2189**

Capital View Motor Inn ($$)
Drive in to the heart of the city.
✉ **Corner Webb & Thompson streets** ☎ **04 385 0515**

Duxton ($$$)
International standard, handily placed with views over the harbor.
✉ **148 Wakefield Street**
☎ **04 473 3900**

Hotel Raffaele ($$$)
Waterfront boutique hotel.
✉ **360 Oriental Parade, Oriental Bay** ☎ **04 384 3450**

InterContinental ($$$)
Central international hotel.
✉ **Grey Street** ☎ **04 472 2722**

James Cook Hotel Grand Chancellor ($$$)
Downtown business and tourist hotel.
✉ **147 The Terrace**
☎ **04 499 9500**

Portland Hotel of Thorndon ($$)
Centrally located, 107 units.
✉ **24 Hawkestone Street, Thorndon** ☎ **04 473 2208**

Trekkers Hotel/Motel ($$)
Budget accommodations with facility and non-facility rooms, and motel units.
✉ **213 Cuba Street**
☎ **04 385 2153**

West Plaza Hotel ($$$)
Centrally located; 102 rooms.
✉ **110–116 Wakefield Street**
☎ **04 473 1440**

Napier

Edgewater Motor Lodge ($$)
Motel-style, adjacent to city center and promenade. Rooms vary from studio units to executive suites, saltwater plunge pool, laundry, and games room.
✉ **359 Marine Parade** ☎ **06 835 1148**

Kennedy Park Accommodation ($)
Motels, tourist flats, cabins, and campsites in suburban park-like grounds.
✉ **Storkey Street** ☎ **06 843 9126**

The Master's Lodge ($$)
Very small upmarket lodge on Bluff Hill with superb views.
✉ **10 Elizabeth Road, Bluff Hill**
☎ **06 834 1946**

Tennyson Motor Inn ($$)
Central city location; 42 units.
✉ **Corner Clive Square & Tennyson Street** ☎ **06 835 3373**

New Plymouth

Amber Court Motel ($$)
Five minutes' walk to city center and close to Pukekura Park, 32 units with kitchens, heated pool.
✉ **61 Eliot Street**
☎ **06 758 0922**

Devon Hotel ($$)
Centrally located with 100 rooms.
✉ **390 Devon Street East**
☎ **06 759 9099**

Flamingo Motel ($$)
A New Zealand Automobile Association award-winner with 30 self-contained units.
✉ **355 Devon Street West**
☎ **06 758 8149**

Motels
Motels in New Zealand are generally a most acceptable form of accommodations. They usually have kitchen (self-catering) facilities in each room unit rather than a central dining room, although breakfast may be provided to units on request.

Upper South Island

Holiday Parks
The term holiday park usually indicates a camping ground for both tents and motorhomes and there are usually a number of cabins and/or tourist apartments for rent as well. Guests may be required to provide their own bed-linen, cutlery, and utensils. Facilities such as washing rooms and lighting range from the basic to the quite luxurious.

Christchurch
Copthorne Durham Street($$)
One of three Quality chain properties in Christchurch.
✉ **Corner Durham & Kilmore streets** ☎ **03 365 4699**

Latimer Hotel ($$)
Ninety units, including 40 new luxury suites, in walking distance of downtown.
✉ **30 Latimer Square** ☎ **03 379 6760**

Raceway Motel ($$)
Units with kitchens, handy to station.
✉ **222 Lincoln Road, Addington** ☎ **03 338 0511**

Rydges Christchurch ($$$)
Smart city center hotel.
✉ **Corner Worcester Street & Oxford Terrace** ☎ **03 379 4700**

Spencer Park Holiday ($)
About 300 camp sites, plus apartments, cabins, and lodge.
✉ **Heyders Road, Spencerville** ☎ **03 329 8721**

Stonehurst Backpackers ($)
Dormitory and two-person accommodation, five minutes' walk from city center. Breakfast available.
✉ **241 Gloucester Street** ☎ **03 379 4620**

Sudima Hotel Grand Chancellor ($$$)
Near the airport; 156 rooms.
✉ **Memorial Avenue** ☎ **03 358 3139** ✈ **Airport**

Blenheim
Blenheim Country Hotel ($$)
Three minutes' walk from town center.
✉ **Corner Alfred & Henry streets** ☎ **03 578 5079**

Mount Cook
Mount Cook Chalets ($$)
Eighteen units with cooking facilities. Operated in conjunction with The Hermitage.
✉ **Mount Cook Village, South Canterbury** ☎ **03 435 1809**

The Hermitage Hotel ($$$)
Well-established hotel of standing in Mount Cook National Park.
✉ **Mount Cook Village, South Canterbury** ☎ **03 435 1809**

Nelson
AA Motel ($$)
Non-smoking units with kitchen facilities; near city center.
✉ **8 Ajax Avenue** ☎ **03 548 8214**

Copthorne Rutherford Hotel ($$)
High standard of accommodations next to city center. Restaurant and bar.
✉ **Trafalgar Square** ☎ **03 548 2299**

Westland National Park
Fox Glacier Holiday Park ($)
Cabins, apartments and lodge rooms; 800m from township.
✉ **Lake Matheson Road, Fox Glacier** ☎ **03 751 0821**

Franz Josef Glacier Hotel ($$$)
Renovated rooms (147) in Franz Josef township.
✉ **State Highway 6, Franz Josef** ☎ **03 752 0729**

Terrace Motel ($$)
Ten units with kitchen facilities, five minutes' walk to village.
✉ **Cowan Street, Franz Josef Glacier** ☎ **03 752 0130**

Lower South Island

Queenstown

Gardens Parkroyal Hotel ($$$)
On Lake Wakatipu waterfront, adjacent to shopping area.
✉ **Corner Earl Street & Marine Parade** ☎ **03 442 7750**

Garden Court Suites and Apartments ($$)
Forty units with views, 6km from Queenstown.
✉ **41 Frankton Road**
☎ **03 442 9713**

Millennium Queenstown ($$$)
Views of lake and mountains.
✉ **corner Frankton Road & Stanley Street** ☎ **03 441 8888**

Queenstown Motor Park ($)
Campsites, cabins, lodge, apartments.
✉ **51 Man Street**
☎ **03 442 7252**

Rydges Queenstown ($$$)
Well-appointed rooms overlooking lake.
✉ **38–54 Lake Esplanade**
☎ **03 442 7600**

Spinnaker Bay Apartments ($$$)
Luxurious one-, two- and three-bedroom units, with kitchens.
✉ **151 Frankton Road**
☎ **03 442 5050**

St James Apartments ($$)
Quality accommodations in one- and two-bedroom units.
✉ **Coronation Drive**
☎ **03 442 5333**

Dunedin

Abbey Lodge ($$)
Twelve self-contained units and 38 hotel rooms; 2km from city center.
✉ **900 Cumberland Street**
☎ **03 477 5380**

Garden Motel ($$)
Twelve-unit motel with cooking facilities; 2km from city center.
✉ **958 George Street**
☎ **03 477 8251**

Leviathan Hotel ($$)
Near the station; 77 rooms.
✉ **27 Queens Gardens**
☎ **03 477 3160**

Southern Cross Hotel ($$$)
City center location; 134 rooms.
✉ **Corner Princes & High streets** ☎ **03 477 0752**

Invercargill

Ascot Park Hotel ($$)
Seventy hotel rooms and 24 motel units five minutes' drive from city center.
✉ **Corner Tay Street & Racecourse Road**
☎ **03 217 6195**

Surrey Court Motels ($$)
Ten-unit motel with cooking facilities.
✉ **400 Tay Street**
☎ **03 217 6102**

Te Anau

Holiday Inn Te Anau ($$$)
International hotel near lake.
✉ **Lake Front Drive**
☎ **03 249 9700**

Luxmore Hotel Lodge ($$)
Town center hotel.
✉ **Main Street**
☎ **03 249 7526**

Wanaka

Edgewater Resort ($$$)
Rooms (100) with balconies.
✉ **Sargood Drive**
☎ **03 443 8311**

Te Wanaka Lodge ($$)
Luxurious B&B.
✉ **23 Brownston Street**
☎ **03 443 9224**

Booking Ahead

Regardless of your choice of accommodations, remember that the summer season, from October through to April, is the busiest time. Most hotels are full in February and March, and most motels tend to be full in December and January. Booking ahead for these months at least, as well as during New Zealand's school and public holidays (► 116), is advisable.

103

Major Shopping Districts

With or Without Tax?

New Zealand has a Goods and Services Tax (GST) of 12.5 percent applicable to all goods purchased, including food and accommodations. By law this tax is included in the price stated unless otherwise indicated. However, it is always as well to check that the price is inclusive, particularly at some of the more expensive hotels and restaurants. Some of the guided walking tours may also advertise prices without tax.

Auckland and Upper North Island

Auckland's main downtown shopping thoroughfare is Queen Street, running from Queen Elizabeth II Square at the Ferry Building to Aotea Square, with its Aotea Centre and Town Hall. The major hotels, airline offices, banks, stores, postal facilities, central library, art gallery, cinemas, concert halls, and visitor information centers are located on or adjacent to this street.

There are also many suburban shopping precincts in the city, with Newmarket and the St Lukes Mall in the suburb of Mount Albert being of special interest.

In the upper North Island, Rotorua, Taupo, and the Bay of Islands offer interesting stores for visitors, despite being relatively unknown for shopping.

Wellington and Lower North Island

The capital's main shopping street is Lambton Quay, but Willis Street, Manners Street, and Cuba Street are also of interest, with partial mall development. There is an underground shopping center at the corner of Lambton Quay and Willis Street. Post offices, banks, libraries, theaters, and visitor information centers are close by.

Napier offers a smart downtown shopping area, including some traffic-free streets.

In New Plymouth shopping is centered on its main street (Devon Street), part of which is traffic-restricted. One block north, the City Centre Mall offers enclosed shopping.

Christchurch and Upper South Island

Cathedral Square marks the center of downtown Christchurch, with Colombo Street and Cashel Street (City Mall) being the main shopping thoroughfares. Other side streets are also of interest, however. Commercial facilities, including post offices and banks, are also in this area.

To the north of the square, in Colombo Street, there are many tourist and souvenir shops and a visitor information office is situated in Cathedral Square.

Christchurch's largest suburban shopping area is at Riccarton, where there is both street-side and mall shopping.

In the upper South Island, Nelson has a colorful shopping area.

Queenstown and Lower South Island

Queenstown is a major tourist center and most shops in its compact downtown area are geared towards visitors. It is also the only place in New Zealand where major stores and boutiques stay open until 10PM daily.

Dunedin, a city with a much larger resident population, has many good shops in George and Princes streets, on either side of the Octagon reserve.

Invercargill has a modest downtown shopping area.

The small towns of Te Anau and Wanaka, have fairly limited shopping. However, both these shopping areas offer interesting browsing for travelers.

Department & Clothing Stores

Auckland

Canterbury of New Zealand
New Zealand clothing, specializing in smart/ casual wear.
✉ 163 Broadway, Newmarket
☎ 09 520 0755

Kathmandu
Popular New Zealand clothing label, specializing in outdoor wear.
✉ 151 Queen Street
☎ 09 309 4615

Rodd & Gunn
High-quality outdoor clothing.
✉ 75 Queen Street (and branches) ☎ 09 309 6571

Saks
A fashionable store for exclusive men's and women's clothing.
✉ 254 Broadway, Newmarket
☎ 09 520 7630

Smith & Caughey's
Fine department store, including fashion.
✉ 253–261 Queen Street
☎ 09 377 4770

Victoria Park Market
Arts, crafts, and cafés.
✉ Victoria Street West

Wellington

Beders
European and New Zealand fashion.
✉ Capital on the Quay, 226–256 Lambton Quay
☎ 04 472 8315

Destiny Extreme Sports
Sports equipment and gear.
✉ 55 Cuba Street
☎ 04 499 8963

Kirkcaldie & Stains Ltd
Elegant department store near the waterfront.
✉ 165–177 Lambton Quay
☎ 04 472 5899

Leder
Leather clothes and accessories.
✉ 195 Lambton Quay
☎ 04 499 6670

Christchurch

Ballantynes
Popular department store with large variety of merchandise.
✉ City Mall, 130 Cashel Street
☎ 03 379 7400

Hallensteins
Smart menswear at moderate prices.
✉ 137 Cashel Street
☎ 03 366 4169

Milano Men
Menswear fashion clothing, both imported and local.
✉ Guthrey Centre, 79 Cashel Street Mall ☎ 03 365 5409

Quinns Fashions
Quality labels at higher prices.
✉ Merivale Mall, 185 Papanui Road, Merivale ☎ 03 355 7349

Queenstown

Canterbury of New Zealand
New Zealand clothing, specializing in smart/ casual wear.
✉ O'Connells Shopping Centre ☎ 03 442 4020

T and Ski Originals
Kiwi-style leisurewear.
✉ The Mall & Steamer Wharf
☎ 03 442 9817

Dunedin

Arthur Barnett Ltd
Older, established department store with an array of ladies' and men's clothing, household furnishings, and giftware.
✉ 267 George Street
☎ 03 477 1129

Chain Stores
In New Zealand, the Woolworths name is applied to a chain of grocery supermarkets. The Warehouse chain operates as a discount operation, with a wide variety of general merchandise. Most cities and towns also have a Farmers store, offering a large range of household goods and clothing. K-Mart stores, selling similar stock, are found in many major suburbs and towns.

New Zealand Labels
Internationally recognized New Zealand labels are always in demand. Canterbury brand clothing is popular. Swanndri and Kathmandu are two recognized outdoor clothing labels. Zeal, Hot Buttered, and Origin are other New Zealand labels sought by the young at heart. Karen Walker, World, Zambesi, and Moontide are top labels for fashion-conscious women.

Books, Magazines & Music

Bookshops

Whitcoulls have branches in all cities and major suburbs. Paper Plus is a franchise chain. The larger cities usually have a number of specialist bookstores carrying selected subjects. Second-hand bookshops in towns tend to stock mainly paperbacks, whereas in the larger cities second-hand hardbacks can also be found.

Music Shops

All towns have one or more stores selling CDs and cassettes. As well as the usual range, Maori and Polynesian music are available in both formats. Sounds is a chain of music stores in many North Island locations. Records are not widely sold, but second-hand records, along with used cassettes and CDs, can be found in the country's three main cities.

Books and Magazines

Auckland

Dorothy Butler Bookshop
Children's books and crafts.
✉ **Corner Jervois & St Marys Bay Road, Ponsonby**
☏ **09 376 7283**

Dymocks
Main Auckland store for large Australian bookseller.
✉ **Atrium on Elliott, 21 Elliott Street** ☏ **09 379 9919**

Parsons
Specialist books on the arts and New Zealand.
✉ **New Gallery Building, Wellesley Sreet** ☏ **09 303 1557**

Pathfinder
Specialist bookstore for psychology and well-being.
✉ **New Gallery Building, Wellesley Street**
☏ **09 379 0147**

Rare Books
One of Auckland's better stores for used non-fiction.
✉ **6 High Street**
☏ **09 379 0379**

Wellington

Arty Bee's
Popular second-hand bookstore.
✉ **17 Courtenay Place**
☏ **04 385 1819**

Bennetts
Book store for government and New Zealand publications, affiliated with Whitcoulls chain.
✉ **Bowen House, corner Lambton Quay & Bowen Street**
☏ **04 499 3433**

Unity Books
Specialist retailer for arts and intellectual titles.
✉ **57 Willis Street**
☏ **04 499 4245**

Christchurch

Scorpio Books
Mainly, but not exclusively, arts and serious topics.
✉ **79 Hereford Street**
☏ **03 379 2882**

UBS University Book Shop
For both students and public; a wide selection of topics.
✉ **University Drive, Ilam**
☏ **03 348 8579**

CDs and Cassettes

Auckland

Marbecks
Auckland's top store for serious listening.
✉ **15 Queens Arcade, 164 Queen Street**
☏ **09 379 0444**

Real Groovy Records
Selection of new and used records, cassettes and CDs.
✉ **438 Queen Street**
☏ **09 302 3940**

Wellington

Allan's Compact Discs Ltd
General catalogue of most popular and classical works.
✉ **AA Centre, 342–352 Lambton Quay** ☏ **04 499 0675**

Parsons Books & Music
A serious bookshop with classical CDs as well.
✉ **126 Lambton Quay**
☏ **04 472 4587**

Christchurch

Echo Records
New and used CDs and cassettes.
✉ **237 High Street**
☏ **03 366 7410**

Dunedin

Disk Den
All types of CDs and cassettes.
✉ **118 Princes Street**
☏ **03 477 2280**

Handcrafts, Antiques & Markets

Auckland

Downtown Hilton Gallery
Paintings, especially those featuring New Zealand scenery.
✉ **Downtown Shopping Centre, 4 Albert Street**
☎ **09 303 3836**

Elephant House Crafts
Selling a variety of craft items you didn't think you needed!
✉ **237 Parnell Road, Parnell**
☎ **09 309 8740**

International Art Centre
Art by famous artists.
✉ **272 Parnell Road, Parnell**
☎ **09 379 4010**

Otara Market
Open-air early morning market with vegetables, domestic items and general merchandise. Some are second-hand.
✉ **Newbury Lane, Otara**
🕐 **Sat only**

Victoria Park Market
A permanent collection of little shops and stallholders housed in an old converted building several blocks from the downtown area. Offers a varied selection of arts, crafts, cafés, and casual clothing.
✉ **Victoria Street West**

Wellington

McGregor Wright Gallery
Art dealers specializing mostly in 20th-century New Zealand artists.
✉ **Law Society Building, 26 Waring Taylor Street**
☎ **04 472 1281**

The Market
Various stalls and a food hall.
✉ **James Smith building, corner Cuba & Manners streets**

Wellington Market
Over 150 stalls from Friday through Sunday.
✉ **Corner of Taranaki Street & Jervois Quay**

Walker & Hall Antiques
A jeweler and silversmith. Branches in Auckland and Christchurch as well.
✉ **148 Lambton Quay**
☎ **04 473 9266**

Christchurch

Arts Centre
A variety of stores selling arts, crafts, and souvenirs all housed in a classic Gothic building. At weekends there are also a number of outside stallholders.
✉ **Worcester Boulevard**

Galleria and Arts Centre Workshop
Includes Maori carvings and handcrafted glassware.
✉ **Arts Centre, Worcester Street** ☎ **03 366 0989**

Not Just Bears
Huge selection of classic and modern teddy bears for you to choose from.
✉ **73 Victoria Street**
☎ **03 377 1311**

Queenstown

Central Art Galleries
Quality fine arts.
✉ **Beach Street**
☎ **03 442 7025**

Queenstown Gallery
New Zealand fine art.
✉ **61 Lower Beach Street**
☎ **03 441 1366**

Dunedin

Rosslyn Gallery
Local original art and reproductions.
✉ **320 George Street**
☎ **03 477 9899**

Antiques
True antiques are rare in New Zealand and most items regarded as antique are in fact only between 40 and 80 years old. The terms second-hand and antique tend to be used rather loosely and often a good deal of the former has to be sifted through before anything of value can be found.

English dinner sets, Victorian bric-à-brac, and art of all kinds are sought-after and popular collectors' items include small toys, cigarette cards, jewelry, and ginger jars.

Tourist Souvenirs

Souvenirs
Generally, souvenirs of New Zealand reflect its Maori culture, its agricultural heritage, and its scenery. Handcrafted items are prevalent and there are good selections of pottery, paintings, Maori-designed woodcarvings, greenstone (jade) jewelry, sheepskin rugs, woollen ware, honey, wine, placemats, books, and calendars of scenic photos.

Lucky Charm
The *hei-tiki*, more often known simply as the *tiki*, is a favorite Maori souvenir. Thought possibly to have originated as a fertility symbol, its true significance has been lost in time. These days it is widely sold as a small good-luck charm, carved from either greenstone or wood.

Auckland
Aotea NZ Souvenirs
The Auckland branch of a nationwide chain.
✉ Lower Albert Street
☎ 09 379 5022

Artport
New Zealand art at the airport.
✉ Auckland International Airport ☎ 09 256 8087

Auckland Museum Gift Shop
Rated as one of Auckland's best souvenir shops.
✉ Auckland Domain, Parnell
☎ 09 309 2580

Auckland Tourist Centre Souvenirs
Located downtown at the terminal for airport buses.
✉ Downtown Airline Terminal, 86 Quay Street
☎ 09 379 6289

Exclusively New Zealand
Central city location.
✉ 34 Queen Street
☎ 09 309 5642

Souvenirs of New Zealand
Jewelry, woollen products. 30 minutes south of Auckland.
✉ 229 Great South Road, Takanini
☎ 09 299 8450

Wellington
Great New Zealand Shop
Covers a wide selection – sheepskin rugs, knitwear.
✉ AMP Centre, Grey Street
☎ 04 472 6817

Christchurch
Aotea NZ Souvenirs
The Christchurch branch of a nationwide chain.
✉ 65 Cathedral Square
☎ 03 366 7814

Leather Image
Large selection of leather jackets.
✉ 34 Fitzgerald Avenue
☎ 03 365 3007

Woodcraft Gallery
Offers a variety of fine wood-turned and handcrafted items.
✉ Arts Centre ☎ 03 365 6082

Queenstown
Alpine Artifacts
Choose from a variety of local souvenirs, including clothing.
✉ 34 Queenstown Mall
☎ 03 442 8649

Aotea NZ Souvenirs
For all kinds of New Zealand souvenirs.
✉ 1 Beach Street
☎ 03 442 6444

Dunedin
Glendermid
Lambskin rugs, woollen slippers, travel rugs, and handbags.
✉ 192 Castle Street
☎ 03 477 3655

New Zealand Shop
All types of souvenirs of New Zealand origin, which can be posted around the world.
✉ 6 Civic Centre, Octagon
☎ 03 477 3379

Otago Museum Shop & Craft Gallery
New Zealand crafts and souvenirs.
✉ 419 Great King Street
☎ 03 474 7474

The Scottish Shop
The place in Dunedin to buy all things Scottish.
✉ 17 George Street
☎ 03 477 9965

Tourist Information

All cities and towns have an office belonging to the Visitor Information Network, operated locally, which can provide information about and usually make bookings for attractions, tours, transport, and accommodations. The offices are signposted nationally with the symbol ℹ️.

All national parks have a visitor center run by the Department of Conservation (DoC) with information about the geography, geology, environment, flora, and fauna on display. The center also provides details about what can be done and seen in each park, including walking routes.

The head office of the New Zealand Automobile Association is located at 99 Albert Street, Auckland. There are also a number of other offices throughout the country.

Visitor Information Offices

Upper North Island

Auckland
✉️ Aotea Square, 287 Queen Street ☎ 09 979 2333

Bay Of Islands
✉️ Marsden Road, Paihia
☎ 09 402 7345

Rotorua
✉️ 1167 Fenton Street
☎ 07 348 5179

Taupo
✉️ 30 Tongariro Street
☎ 07 376 0027

Lower North Island

Napier
✉️ Marine Parade
☎ 06 834 1911

New Plymouth
✉️ Corner Liardet & Leach streets ☎ 06 758 6080

Wellington
✉️ 101 Wakefield Street
☎ 04 802 4860; also on Inter-island ferries operating from Wellington to Picton

Upper South Island

Christchurch
✉️ Old Chief Post Office, Cathedral Square
☎ 03 379 9629

Mount Cook
✉️ Bowen Drive
☎ 03 435 1186

Nelson
✉️ Corner Trafalgar & Halifax streets ☎ 03 548 2304

Picton
✉️ The Foreshore
☎ 03 573 7477

Westland National Park
✉️ SH6, Franz Josef village
☎ 03 752 0796; also at Fox Glacier ☎ 03 751 0807

Lower South Island

Dunedin
✉️ 48 The Octagon
☎ 03 474 3300

Invercargill
✉️ c/o Southland Museum, Queens Park ☎ 03 214 6243

Queenstown
✉️ Corner Shotover & Camp streets ☎ 03 442 4100

Te Anau
✉️ Lake Front Drive
☎ 03 249 8900

Wanaka
✉️ Ardmore Street
☎ 03 443 1233

Photographic Film

Major brands of photographic film can be bought nationwide. Processing of color prints, with a price structure related to the time taken, is also undertaken at many places. The processing of slide film is not so widespread and film will probably have to be forwarded to an appropriate laboratory.

North Island

Amusements Galore
As well as purpose-built attractions, there are numerous parks and playgrounds in New Zealand, together with plenty of cinemas, video-game parlors, bowling alleys, go-kart tracks, and all sorts of other modern pastimes. However, remember that whatever children are up to in the open air, they (and you!) should always be well protected from the sun.

Auckland
Auckland Zoo
Always a favorite with children, especially the elephants, lions, and hippos.
✉ **Motions Road, Western Springs** ☎ **09 360 3819** 🕐 **Daily 9:30-5:30; last admission 4:15**

Glenbrook Vintage Railway
Steam train rides on summer Sundays, from Glenbrook towards Waiuku.
✉ **50km south of Auckland** ☎ **09 636 9361** 🕐 **Hourly departures, 11-4**

Kelly Tarlton's Underwater World and Antarctic Experience
Fish, sharks, and penguins will entertain young and old alike.
✉ **Tamaki Drive, Orakei** ☎ **09 528 0603** 🕐 **9-6 in winter, 9-8 summer; last admission 5/7**

Rainbow's End Adventure Park
New Zealand's best-known leisure park.
✉ **Wiri Station Road, Manukau** ☎ **09 262 2030** 🕐 **Daily; not evenings**

Waiwera
Hot thermal swimming pools and hydro-slides.
✉ **Waiwera Road; 48km north of Auckland on SH1** ☎ **09 427 8800** 🕐 **Daily 9AM-10PM**

Hastings
Splash Planet
Water-based children's playground.
✉ **Grove Road** ☎ **06 876 9856** 🕐 **Daily**

Napier
Lilliput Model Railway
Working model town.

✉ **Marineland, Marine Parade** ☎ **06 834 4027** 🕐 **10-4:30**

Marineland of New Zealand
Sealife and shows.
✉ **Marine Parade** ☎ **06 834 4027** 🕐 **Daily 10-4:30; shows at 10:30 and 2**

National Aquarium of New Zealand
Displays of native and exotic species.
✉ **Marine Parade** ☎ **06 834 1404** 🕐 **9-6, later in summer; feeding at 10 and 2**

Rotorua
Rainbow Farm
Farm animals.
✉ **Fairy Springs Road, opposite Rainbow Springs** ☎ **07 350 0440** 🕐 **8-5; farm shows at 10:30, 11:45, 1, 2:30 and 4**

Skyline Luge
Ride up by gondola, and then descend by luge sledge on a special pathway.
✉ **Fairy Springs Road** ☎ **07 347 0027** 🕐 **Winter 9-6, summer 9-8 or later**

Toot and Whistle Railway
Train rides round Kuirau Park.
✉ **Corner Ranolf & Pukuatua streets** ☎ **07 348 4133** 🕐 **Weekends and public holidays**

Taupo
AC Baths
Modernised hot mineral pools, with hydroslides.
✉ **Corner AC Baths & Spa roads** ☎ **07 376 0340**

Aratiatia Rapids
Water is diverted across the rocks of the old riverbed.
✉ **Aratiatia Power Station Dam, north of Wairakei** ☎ **0800 820 082** 🕐 **At 10, noon and 2 (also 4 in summer)**

South Island

Christchurch
Air Force Museum
Aeroplanes and all sorts of other aviation items.
✉ Air Force Museum, Main South Road, Wigram
☎ 03 343 9532 ⏲ 10–5

Christchurch Gondola
Ride up the Port Hills and visit the Time Tunnel at the summit.
✉ Bridle Path Road, Heathcote ☎ 03 384 0700
⏲ From 10AM

International Antarctic Centre
Interesting display, including movies. A souvenir shop is also available.
✉ Orchard Road, next to the airport ☎ 03 353 7798
⏲ Daily 9:30–5:30; to 8:30PM in summer

Orana Wildlife Park
African and native animals in natural settings.
✉ McLeans Island Road, Harewood ☎ 03 359 7109
⏲ 10–5

Science Alive!
A hands-on display in the former railroad station.
✉ Moorhouse Avenue, about 1km from Cathedral Square
☎ 03 365 5199

Dunedin
Discovery World
A hands-on science center of special interest to children.
✉ Otago Museum, Great King Street ☎ 03 477 2372
⏲ Daily 10–5

Ocean Beach Railway
Steam-train rides weekends and public holidays.
✉ St Kilda Beach ☎ 03 474 3300 (visitor information)
⏲ Times vary

Taieri Gorge Train
A four-hour round-trip through the Taieri Gorge, departing every afternoon.
✉ Dunedin Station
☎ 03 477 4449

Mount Cook
Glentanner Park
Farm tours, horse treks, safaris and snow excursions.
✉ SH 80 leading in to Mt Cook
☎ 03 435 1855

Nelson
World of Wearable Art & Collectable Cars
Fantastic 'clothes' and wonderful cars.
✉ 95 Quarantine Road, Annesbrook ☎ 03 548 9299

Queenstown
Jet-boat Rides
The most popular is the Shotover Jet, but there are other, cheaper options.
✉ Pick-ups from downtown
☎ 03 442 8570
⏲ Every 15 minutes

Queenstown Underwater World
Step under the water level and view the marine life.
✉ Queenstown wharf (foot of The Mall) ☎ 03 442 8437
⏲ 9–5:30 (to 7PM in summer)

Skyline Gondola
Take the cableway up above the city.
✉ Base station in Brecon Street ☎ 03 441 0101 ⏲ 9–10

Westland National Park
Glowworm Grotto
A short bush walk shows glowworm insect lights on banks and under bushes. Visit at night and take a torch.
✉ Near Fox Glacier village on SH6 ☎ 03 751 0807

Child Prices
Most of the attractions listed here and elsewhere in the book offer cheaper entrance fees for children. The upper age limits vary: sometimes 12 years, sometimes 16 years.

Some transport and attractions operators also recognize International Student Identity Cards and Youth Hostels Association (YHA) membership cards.

Culture &
Entertainment

Parades
Teams of marching girls in colorful costumes are a familiar sight in New Zealand. The country's Scottish heritage is shown in the many pipe bands to be seen, and there are also many brass bands. Parades are conjured up for any event or occasion, ranging from Christmas to rugby matches.

While the culture of the Maori is unique to New Zealand, classical orchestral music, opera, ballet, and theater are also well represented in the main cities. Outside the towns, the largely agricultural base of New Zeland's economy is reflected in shows of a peculiarly Kiwi type, with farming made into entertainment.

A&P Shows
Distinctly agricultural and pastoral, these shows are held annually around many farming centers. Hamilton, Rotorua, and Queenstown have daily tourist shows featuring farm animals, with displays ranging from milking cows to shearing sheep.

New Zealand's largest show is the National Agricultural Fieldays, held over four days in the second week of June, at Mystery Creek near Hamilton.

Maori Culture
Maori concerts are given nightly in Rotorua, and also regularly in Auckland, Christchurch and Queenstown. The chants and actions of Maori warriors preparing for battle are remembered in the *haka*, while the women's *poi* dance offers a gentler form of entertainment. The *poi* is a light ball on a string which is swung to a rhythmic beat.

Performing Arts
Generally, Auckland, as the largest city, plays host to any major stage performance. Huge outdoors concerts are staged in the Auckland Domain during summer. The city's Pasifika Polynesian

Festival in March is a must.

Wellington, on the other hand, is regarded as the country's cultural capital and its biennial Arts Festival, held in the autumn (February /March) of even-numbered years, is a significant event featuring many famous New Zealand and international artists. Wellington is also home to the New Zealand Symphony Orchestra and the Royal New Zealand Ballet – though both also tour other towns and cities.

Nightlife
Generally, nightclubs cater mostly to younger adults and lack the sophistication and variety of some overseas destinations. Casinos are located in Auckland, Hamilton, Christchurch, Dunedin and Queenstown. Many taverns and bars provide live music, including jazz.

The student population of the university cities of Auckland, Wellington, Christchurch, Dunedin, Hamilton, and Palmerston North helps keep the night entertainment scene alive.

Queenstown, the country's leading ski resort, offers a variety of après-ski events during the winter.

Sport
Rugby is the most popular winter sport and is considered the national game. Cricket and lawn bowls are the most popular summer sports. Bush-walking and swimming are favored leisure activities.

The popularity of sport with New Zealanders means that it is an essential part of the country's culture (▶ 114).

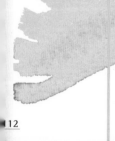

Cultural Activities

North Island

Auckland

Auckland Central City Library

The country's largest public library has an excellent collection of New Zealand, Maori, Pacific Island and European rare books.

✉ Lorne Street, City ☎ 09 377 0209 🕐 Mon–Fri 9:30–8, Sat 10–4, Sun noon–4

Auckland Museum

Offers a daily display of Maori song and dance at 11, 12 and 1:30, and 2:30 in summer.

✉ Auckland Domain, Cenotaph Road; 3km from downtown ☎ 09 306 7067

Bruce Mason Theatre

A modern venue, with a variety of local activities.

✉ 1 The Promenade, Takapuna ☎ 09 488 2940

Civic Theatre

One of the southern hemisphere's most ornate movie houses, opened in 1929.

✉ Corner Queen & Wellesley streets ☎ 09 377 3315

New Plymouth

Govett-Brewster Art Gallery

Known for its contemporary paintings and kinetic sculptures.

✉ Queen Street ☎ 06 758 5149 🕐 Daily 10:30–5

Rotorua

New Zealand Maori Arts and Crafts Institute

Display of Maori song and dance at 12:15 every weekday, plus other Maori crafts.

✉ Hemo Road ☎ 07 348 9047 🕐 Daily 8–5

Tamaki Tours

An evening tour combining a *hangi* dinner and a Maori song and dance show in a reconstructed village setting.

✉ Depart from Visitor Centre, Fenton Street ☎ 07 346 2823

Wellington

Downstage Theatre

Regarded as Wellington's best playhouse.

✉ Hannah Playhouse, Courtenay Place ☎ 04 801 6946

Dowse Art Museum

One of the best art galleries in the Wellington region.

✉ Laings Road, Lower Hutt ☎ 04 570 6500 🕐 10–4 Mon–Fri, Sat–Sun and holidays 11–5

Michael Fowler Centre

The leading concert venue in Wellington.

✉ Wakefield Street ☎ 04 801 4242

New Zealand Symphony Orchestra

The orchestra performs frequently at the Michael Fowler Centre.

✉ Wakefield Street ☎ 04 801 3890

South Island

Christchurch

Christchurch Town Hall

A concert chamber and theater with frequent activity, including a local orchestra.

✉ Kilmore Street ☎ 03 377 8899

Court Theatre

Good productions of plays and light shows, six nights a week.

✉ Arts Centre, 20 Worcester Street ☎ 03 366 6992

Television

The four national television channels are known as One, 2, TV3 and TV4. Both 2 and TV4 provide light entertainment, aimed at the younger market, while One and TV3 concentrate on current affairs and sport. All channels feature commercials.

There are also a number of regional channels. Sky Television is the major subscriber network and is shown in most major hotels and better motels.

Outdoor Activities

National Favorites
Rugby is New Zealand's number one competitive sport and the national team, the All Blacks, is known internationally. Other popular winter sports include netball, soccer and hockey.

In summer, cricket takes the limelight nationally, and lawn bowls is also a favorite. Horse-racing and trotting (harness-racing) meetings, which attract large crowds, are held most weekends at tracks through the country.

Adventure Sports
New Zealand offers a wide variety of popular adventure and thrill activities, such as jet-boating, bungy-jumping, para-gliding, and white-water rafting. While Queenstown is the home for many of these activities, several are available in other centers.

The South Island's Southern Alps mountain chain offers many climbing and mountaineering opportunities, requiring varying degrees of skill.

Boating
This is a favorite Kiwi pastime. You can go cruising in the harbors and gulf of Auckland, the Bay of Islands, the Marlborough Sounds, the lakes of Rotorua, or the lakes and fiords of the south.

Fishing
The Rotorua and Taupo areas are famous for trout whereas parts of the South Island south of Christchurch are better known for salmon fishing. South Island rivers are also famous for trout, but you need a license to fish.

Fishing trips, including deep-sea game fishing, are available from Paihia, Russell. Tutukaka, and Northland.

Golf
Golf courses are found everywhere. In Rotorua and Taupo, thermal vents can be unusual hazards. The Wairakei International Golf Course 8km north of Taupo is recognized as one of the world's best.

Horse-racing
Ellerslie Racecourse in Auckland is the city's premier racetrack. Meetings are held about every second or third Saturday; more often at holiday times. There is also trotting (harness-racing) at Alexandra Park, although Addington, in the South Island; is considered the home of trotting. The main events in Christchurch for both horse-trotting and racing are during Carnival week in November.

Skiing
The North Island's major ski-fields (July to September, sometimes longer) are on the northern and southwestern slopes of Mount Ruapehu in Tongariro National Park.

Coronet Peak and the Remarkables are Queenstown's two major ski-fields. There are more located near Wanaka. The city of Christchurch also has a number of private and club fields within two hours' drive.

Walking
The extensive and varied types of countryside offers many walking tracks. Details of escorted walks or routes are available from the national park centers. Seek local advice before setting off alone, let someone know you are going, and always carry warm, all-weather clothing, food, and maps.

Watersports
Watersports of all kinds can be found throughout New Zealand, either along the extensive coast or on inland lakes and rivers. For the less energetic, swimming in the country's hot thermal springs is a pleasant option.

The Bay of Islands offers diving and snorkeling.

Evening Entertainment

Auckland

Abby's
Live music.
✉ **Corner of Wellesley & Albert streets** ☎ **09 303 4799**

Bass
For hip-hop and R&B fans.
✉ **10 Victoria Street**
☎ **09 379 7897**

Civic Tavern
Offers London, Irish and Tartan bars, plus jazz several nights a week.
✉ **Corner of Queen & Wellesley streets** ☎ **09 373 3684**

Coast
Sophisticated, stylish bar and lounge.
✉ **Level 7, Hewlett Packard Building, Princes Wharf**
☎ **09 300 9966**

Sky City Casino
The largest casino in New Zealand.
✉ **Corner of Victoria & Federal streets** ☎ **09 363 6000**

Stanley's Bar and Nightclub
Disco for the more mature nightclubber.
✉ **192 Queen Street, Central Auckland** ☎ **09 309 0201**

The Loaded Hog
Lively pub, serving meals, located next to the yacht basin.
✉ **204 Quay Street**
☎ **09 366 6491**

Wellington

Kitty O'Shea's Irish Bar
Live Irish music.
✉ **28 Courtenay Place**
☎ **04 384 7392**

The Planet Bar and Cafe
Entertainment through to the early hours.
✉ **Corner of Courtenay Place & Tory Street**
☎ **04 382 9747**

Rotorua

The Ace of Clubs
Late-night disco from Wednesday to Saturday.
✉ **Ti Street** ☎ **07 346 2204**

Christchurch

Christchurch Casino
Poker machines and gambling tables, plus a restaurant and bars.
✉ **30 Victoria Street**
☎ **03 365 9999**

Sammy's Jazz Review
Lively jazz club.
✉ **14 Bedford Row**
☎ **03 377 8618**

Queenstown

McNeills Cottage Brewery
A boutique brewery and restaurant.
✉ **14 Church Street**
☎ **03 442 9688**

Sky Alpine Queenstown Casino
Small and intimate.
✉ **16–24 Beach Street**
☎ **03 441 0400**

Dunedin

Eureka Bar & Café
For eating and drinking, near the university.
✉ **116 Albany Street**
☎ **03 477 7977**

Ruby in the Dust
Live music in city-center location.
✉ **6 The Octagon**
☎ **03 477 4690**

Woolshed Bar & Grill
Lively student bar.
✉ **318 Moray Place**
☎ **03 477 3246**

Live Music
Many New Zealand taverns and public bars feature live music in the form of a trio of electric guitars and drums. The volume is usually very loud. Jazz, less commonly, can also be found. Altogether more sedate is the music played by a pianist in a handful of restaurants and some hotel lounges. Discos are numerous in the main cities.

What's On When

School Holidays

Summer: mid-December to late January
April: first two weeks
Mid-term: two weeks from late June to early July
September: last two weeks

Further Information

For more detailed information on New Zealand, including upcoming events, and to help plan your itinerary, visit the Tourism New Zealand's website at: www.newzealand.com

National Public Holidays

New Year (1 and 2 January)
Waitangi Day: national day (6 February)
Good Friday
Easter Monday
Anzac Day: memorial day for war dead (25 April)
Queen's Birthday (first Monday in June)
Labour Day (fourth Monday in October)
Christmas Day (25 December)
Boxing Day (26 December)

Most stores and attractions are closed on Christmas Day, Good Friday, and the morning of Anzac Day. Tourist amenities are usually open on the other public holidays.

There are also regional holidays which correspond to the founding days of each of the country's 13 provinces.
The main ones are :
Wellington region: third Monday in January.
Auckland, Bay of Islands, Rotorua and Taupo: fourth Monday in January.
Christchurch: during Carnival Week in November.
Queenstown and Dunedin: third Monday in March.

Annual Events and Festivals

January

Auckland: Yachting Regatta (fourth Monday in January). The world's largest sailing regatta is held on Auckland harbor.

February

Marlborough: BMW Wine Marlborough Festival at Blenheim (second or third weekend of February).

February/March

Wellington: Biennial (in even years) International Festival of the Arts.

March

Hokitika: Wild Foods Festival
Masterton: Golden Shears Sheep Shearing Competition.

Easter

Hastings: Highland Games.

April

Wanaka: Warbirds over Wanaka aviation show (in odd years).

June

Hamilton: National Agricultural Fieldays are being held over four days at Mystery Creek; this is one of the world's largest agricultural shows (second week of the month).
Queenstown: the ski season opens with the Fun Festival in the second half of June.

September

Alexandra: Blossom Festival.
Nelson: Wearable Art Festival.

October

New Plymouth: Rhododendron Festival takes place for a fortnight in October.

November

Auckland: Ellerslie Garden Show for five days (second week).
Christchurch: Show Week and horse-racing carnival mid-November.
Countrywide: Guy Fawkes evening fireworks on 5 November.

December

Auckland: Domain summer concerts series begins.

Practical Matters

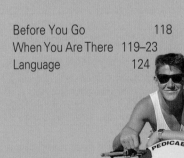

Above: *Flowers of the pohutukawa tree*
Right: *Auckland pedicab*

TIME DIFFERENCES

GMT
12 noon

New Zealand
12 midnight

Germany
→ 1PM

USA (NY)
← 7AM

Netherlands
→ 1PM

Spain
→ 1PM

BEFORE YOU GO

WHAT YOU NEED

	Required ● Suggested ○ Not required ▲ Some countries require a passport to remain valid for a minimum period (usually at least six months) beyond the date of entry – contact their consulate or embassy or your travel agency for details.	UK	Germany	USA	Netherlands	Spain
Passport (must be valid for 3 months beyond period of stay)		●	●	●	●	●
Visa (for holiday travel up to 3 months – check before travelling)		▲	▲	▲	▲	▲
Onward or Round-trip Ticket		●	●	●	●	●
Health Inoculations		▲	▲	▲	▲	▲
Health Documentation (► 123, Health)		○	○	○	○	○
Travel Insurance		○	○	○	○	○
Driving License (national)		●	●	●	●	●
Car Insurance Certificate (included if car is rented)		▲	▲	▲	▲	▲
Car Registration Document		▲	▲	▲	▲	▲

WHEN TO GO

Auckland

High season

Low season

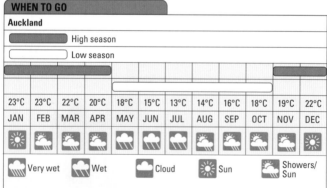

23°C	23°C	22°C	20°C	18°C	15°C	13°C	14°C	16°C	18°C	19°C	22°C
JAN	FEB	MAR	APR	MAY	JUN	JUL	AUG	SEP	OCT	NOV	DEC

Very wet   Wet   Cloud   Sun   Showers/Sun

TOURIST OFFICES

In the UK
Tourism New Zealand
New Zealand House
80 Haymarket
London SW1Y 4TQ
☎ 09069 101010 (recorded information charged at £1 per minute)

In the USA
Tourist New Zealand
Suite 300, 501 Santa Monica Boulevard
Santa Monica
California
CA90401
☎ 310/395 7480
Fax: 310/395 5453

POLICE 111

FIRE 111

AMBULANCE 111

WHEN YOU ARE THERE

ARRIVING

Most visitors arrive by air, through the three main international airports of Auckland, Wellington, and Christchurch. Auckland is the largest gateway, served by more than 20 airlines. Air New Zealand is the national airline (☎ 09 357 3000).

Auckland, North Island Km to city center	Journey times	
	🚆	N/A
23 km	🚌	40 minutes
	🚕	30 minutes

Christchurch, South Island Km to city center	Journey times	
	🚆	N/A
11 km	🚌	30 minutes
	🚕	20 minutes

MONEY

New Zealand currency is decimal based and divided into dollars and cents. The New Zealand dollar is not tied to any other currency. Coins now in circulation are in denominations of 5, 10, 20, and 50 cents and 1 and 2 dollars. Notes are in denominations of 5, 10, 20, 50, and 100 dollars.
There is no limit to the amount of NZ dollars that may be brought into or taken out of the country.
Credit cards are widely accepted and include Mastercard, Visa, American Express, and Diners Club, and travelers checks can be changed at banks and Change Bureaux in all towns.

TIME

 New Zealand standard time is 12 hours ahead of Greenwich Mean Time (GMT+12). New Zealand's proximity to the International Date Line makes it one of the first countries to see each new day.

CUSTOMS

 YES

There are specific allowances for the import of alcohol, cigarettes and luxury goods into the country for those over 17 years of age:
Alcohol:
  spirits: 1.125L
  wine: 4.5L *or*
  beer: 4.5L
Cigarettes: 200 *or*
Cigars: 50 *or*
Tobacco: 250 grams
Toilet water: not specified

Gifts of combined value of NZ$700 or over should be declared and will be subject to customs duty and Goods and Services Tax.

You will be issued on the flight with Passenger Arrival Papers, including an Agriculture Quarantine form.

 NO

Non-prescription drugs, animal, plant or other food products. New Zealand is strict about protecting its agriculture and the interior of the aircraft may be sprayed on arrival.

CONSULATES

UK	Germany	USA	Netherlands	Spain
☎ 04 924 2888	☎ 09 377 3460	☎ 09 303 2724	☎ 09 379 5399	☎ 09 299 6019

WHEN YOU ARE THERE

TOURIST OFFICES

- **Tourism New Zealand**
  P O Box 95
  Lambton Quay
  Wellington
  ☎ 04 917 5400
  Fax: 04 915 3817

Tourist Offices

- **Auckland**
  287 Queen Street
  Aotea Square
  ☎ 09 979 2333

- **Wellington**
  City Visitor Information
  Centre
  Civic Administration
  Building
  Corner Wakefield and
  Victoria streets
  ☎ 04 802 4860

- **Rotorua**
  Tourism Rotorua Complex
  1167 Fenton Street
  ☎ 07 348 5179

- **Christchurch**
  Information Centre
  Old Chief Post Office,
  Cathedral Square
  ☎ 03 379 9629

Over 70 tourist offices
throughout the country form
the Visitor Information
Network, co-ordinated by
Tourism New Zealand.
Because they are linked in
one network, Visitor
Information Centres can also
access information on areas
other than their own. They
provide an invaluable, up-to-
date service and should be
your first port of call.

NATIONAL HOLIDAYS

J	F	M	A	M	J	J	A	S	O	N	D
2	1	(2)	1(3)		1				1		2

1–2 Jan	New Year
6 Feb	Waitangi Day
Mar/Apr	Good Friday
Mar/Apr	Easter Monday
25 Apr	ANZAC Day
Jun (first Mon)	Queen's Birthday
Oct (fourth Mon)	Labour Day
25 Dec	Christmas Day
26 Dec	Boxing Day

In addition, each of the regions of New Zealand has
an Anniversary day (➤ 116).

Some shops and attractions will be open on all but
Christmas Day, Good Friday, and ANZAC Day.

OPENING HOURS

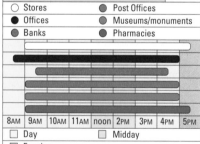

○ Stores	● Post Offices
● Offices	◐ Museums/monuments
◐ Banks	◐ Pharmacies

8AM	9AM	10AM	11AM	noon	2PM	3PM	4PM	5PM

☐ Day	☐ Midday
☐ Evening	

In addition to the above, pharmacies and stores are
open on Saturday 9–noon or 9–4 and some shops are
open on Sunday. The bigger towns usually have late-
night shopping on Thursday or Friday until 8:30 or 9PM.
Some smaller shops close at lunchtime on Saturdays.
Local convenience stores ("dairies") are usually open
7AM - 8PM seven days a week.

Times of museum opening vary and many are open at
weekends, too – for details see individual museums
listed in the What to See section of this guide.

DRIVE ON THE LEFT

TOILETS FREE

PUBLIC TRANSPORT

Internal Flights Air New Zealand and Qantas fly the principal routes within the country and together link about 30 destinations. Both airlines offer an Air Pass scheme which must be bought before traveling to New Zealand but can be open-dated.

Trains Tranz Scenic operates long-distance trains with daily services between the main centers, and the TranzCoastal and TranzAlpine (▶ 24). There are various travel passes available, which allow travel on ferries operated by the railroad, and on Inter City long-distance bus lines. Reservations ☎ 0800 TRAINS.

Coaches and Buses The Inter City long-distance bus network (☎ 09 357 8400) covers much of the country, including many of the tourist areas. Newmans Coachlines operate all major routes, and several com panies offer package tours by long-distance bus.

Ferries The inter-island ferry service is operated by Tranz Rail (☎ 0800 802 802). It is a roll-on roll-off service carrying passeng-ers, motor vehicles, and railroad wagons. There are several round-trip sailings from Wellington to Picton each day, taking 3 hours each way.

Urban Transport Christchurch has a modern heritage tramway system and Auckland has a good bus network, including tourist buses which shuttle around the widely spread attractions of the city. Wellington is a major transport center and ferry terminal, with a cable car from downtown to the upper slopes of the Kelburn area. In some cities bus fares are reduced in off-peak hours Mon–Fri. Cyclists are well provided for.

CAR RENTAL

All the major rental firms are represented in New Zealand. You must be at least 21 to rent a car or motorhome. For inter-island travel, many companies require you to leave the vehicle on one island and pick up another on leaving the ferry. One-way rentals can also be arranged.

TAXIS

Taxis can be hired from ranks; they can also be flagged down. In some towns taxis even offer a rate cheaper than a bus service. For long-distance journeys negotiate the fare in advance. You are not expected to tip taxi drivers.

DRIVING

Speed limits on motorways: **100kph**

Speed limits on main roads: **100kph**

Speed limits on urban roads: **50kph**

Must be worn in all seats where fitted at all times.

Random breath and blood testing. Limit: 80mg of alcohol in 100ml of blood. For drivers under 21 the limit is zero.

Petrol comes in two grades: unleaded 96 octane and unleaded 91 octane. Diesel and LPG (liquefied petroleum gas) are also available. In rural areas service stations may be scarce and may be closed at weekends or outside normal hours. Major centers have 24-hour stations.

There are plenty of motor garages and service stations throughout the country and most rental companies include a free breakdown service as part of the hire package. Automobile Association members receive free reciprocal membership of the New Zealand AA, including breakdown assistance, maps, and accommodations guides (☎ 09 377 4660, Fax: 09 309 4564).

PERSONAL SAFETY

There is an efficient police force modelled on the British system. Police do not carry arms. Whilst New Zealand is generally a safe society, the usual sensible precautions should be taken to ensure personal safety:

- Avoid walking alone in dark areas of towns.
- If walking in bush or mountain country, take good maps, dress sensibly, take supplies of food and drink, and tell someone what your plans are.
- Beware of pickpockets.
- Do not leave valuables in unattended cars.

Police assistance:
☎ **111**
from any call box

TELEPHONES

Telecom operates the public telephone service in New Zealand. Most public call boxes use Telecom phone cards, available in dairies (general stores) and other shops. For directory inquiries dial 018, international directory inquires dial 0172.

International Dialing Codes	
Australia:	00 61
Germany:	00 49
Hong Kong:	00 852
Malaysia:	00 60
Singapore:	00 65
UK:	00 44
USA & Canada:	00 1

POST

Post Offices
The logo for NZ Post Limited is a stylized envelope. It is an efficient service with two grades of post for letters and parcels: Standard Post (2–3 day delivery) and Fastpost (next day delivery). There are Post Shops in most large towns selling stamps, postcards, and stationery.
🕐 Mon–Fri 9–5PM

ELECTRICITY

The power supply in New Zealand is: 230–240 volts AC.

 Sockets accept two or three-flat-pin plugs. Hotels and motels provide 110-volt/20 watt AC sockets for shavers only. An adaptor will be required for those appliances which do not operate on 230 volts.

TIPS/GRATUITIES

Yes ✓   No ✗

Tipping is not generally expected in New Zealand, although it will not be refused if you wish to reward exceptional service.

Restaurants	✗
Tour guides	✗
Hairdressers	✗
Taxi drivers	✗
Chambermaids	✗
Porters	✗
Toilets	✗

What to photograph: New Zealand is immensely photogenic, and the scenery breathtaking. Mountains, geysers, waterfalls and forests, together with Maori culture, make excellent photo subjects.
Best time to photograph: The air is fresh and clear and the light good all year round except, perhaps, when it is raining!
Where to buy film: Film and camera batteries are readily available in shops, pharmacies, airports etc.

HEALTH

Insurance
Some emergency medical services are subsidized for visitors from Australia and the UK, but all visitors are strongly recommended to arrange medical insurance cover in advance of their trip.

Dental Services
All medical, including dental, services are of a high standard and addresses can be found in the front of local telephone directories.

Sun Advice
The most serious potential health risk in New Zealand is from the sun. Ultra-violet radiation throughout the country is particularly high. Take adequate precautions, even on overcast days, by wearing a sun hat and using a sun cream with a high protection factor. Always ensure that children are well protected.

Drugs
Chemists (pharmacies) are usually open during normal shopping hours. If you are on unusual medication, take supplies with you as there is no guarantee that they will be available locally. Take your prescription certificate to avoid difficulties with customs.

Safe Water
Tap water everywhere in New Zealand is safe to drink. City water supplies are chlorinated and most are also fluoridated. If camping in remote areas, always boil water before drinking.

CONCESSIONS

Students/Youths New Zealand caters well for the needs of student and youth travelers. Tranz Scenic, InterCity, Newmans and Tranz Rail have a 30% concession scheme for students on their rail, long-distance bus and ferry services, and Air New Zealand and Qantas have a space-available discount (50%) on internal flights for holders of International Student Identity cards. Youth Hostels Association members receive discounts on InterCity and Newmans.

Senior Citizens Tranz Rail, Tranz Scenic and most long-distance bus operators have a "Golden Age Saver" fare, with a 30% discount on the standard fare for those over 60. You will be required to show proof of your age.

CLOTHING SIZES

New Zealand	UK	Europe	USA	
36	36	46	36	
38	38	48	38	
40	40	50	40	
42	42	52	42	Suits
44	44	54	44	
46	46	56	46	
7	7	41	8	
7.5	7.5	42	8.5	
8.5	8.5	43	9.5	
9.5	9.5	44	10.5	Shoes
10.5	10.5	45	11.5	
11	11	46	12	
14.5	14.5	37	14.5	
15	15	38	15	
15.5	15.5	39/40	15.5	
16	16	41	16	Shirts
16.5	16.5	42	16.5	
17	17	43	17	
8	8	34	6	
10	10	36	8	
12	12	38	10	
14	14	40	12	Dresses
16	16	42	14	
18	18	44	16	
4.5	4.5	38	6	
5	5	38	6.5	
5.5	5.5	39	7	
6	6	39	7.5	Shoes
6.5	6.5	40	8	
7	7	41	8.5	

- There is an airport departure charge of about NZ$25, payable on all international flights. Transit passengers and those under two years of age are exempt.
- There is no limit to the amount of New Zealand currency that may be exported.
- You should arrive at the airport at least two hours before departure time.

LANGUAGE

The common language of New Zealand is English. The written language follows British spelling convention, rather than American. There is little difference in pronunciation from one part of the country to another, except that in the south of the South Island you may detect a Scottish accent. The Maori language is undergoing a revival; you will hear it spoken on a *marae* (the area surrounding a meeting house) and on some radio stations. Visitors may hear Maori spoken on the radio, used as a greeting (*Kia Ora*), and in place names. The language was entirely oral until early missionaries recorded it in written form. The easiest way to say Maori words is to pronounce each syllable phonetically. "Kiwi" English also tends to have its own idiosyncratic expressions or phrases.

🙶 Common Maori Words and Phrases

Ao	cloud
Aotearoa	Land of the Long White Cloud
Ara	path
Atua	god
Awa	river
Haere mai	welcome
Haera ra	farewell
Hangi	a Maori feast
Hau	wind
Hawaiiki	legendary homeland of the Maori
Kia ora	your good health
Kumara	a sweet potato
Makomako	bellbird
Ma	stream
Mana	prestige
Manu	bird
Maunga	mountain
Moana	sea, or lake
Moko	tattoo
Motu	island, or anything that is isolated
Pa	fortified village
Pakeha	foreigner, white person, European
Po	night
Puke	hill
Puna	spring (of water)
Rangi	sky
Roto	lake
Rua	two, eg. Rotorua two lakes
Tapu	sacred
Utu	retribution
Wai	water
Whanga	bay, stretch of water, inlet
Whare	house
Whenua	land

'Kiwi' English

Aussie	Australian
bach	a holiday chalet in the North Island (pronounce 'batch')
Beehive	the main government building in Wellington
bludge	scrounge, borrow
bush	the forest
chook	chicken
cocky	farmer (usually *cow-cocky*)
chilly-bin	portable cooler box
crib	the South Island equivalent of a bach
crook	sick, ill
dag	a character, or entertaining person
dairy	general store
gidday	good day (hello)
good as gold	fine, OK
handle	beer glass with a handle
jandals	flip-flops, thongs
judder bars	speed bumps in the road
morning tea	mid-morning tea or coffee break
mozzie	mosquito
Pakeha	person of European descent
Pom	an English person (mildly derogatory)
smoko	tea or coffee break
togs	swimwear
wopwops	the back of beyond

Acknowledgments

The Automobile Association wishes to thank the following libraries, photographers and associations for their assistance in the preparation of this book:

ALLAN EDIE 122a, 122b, 122c; FOOTPRINTS (Nick Hanna) 7a, 24, 76; MARY EVANS PICTURE LIBRARY 10a, 10b, 14; MRI BANKERS' GUIDE TO FOREIGN CURRENCY 119; TE PAPA TONGAREWA MUSEUM 19

The remaining transparencies are held in the Association's own library (AA PHOTO LIBRARY) and were all taken by Paul Kenward with the exception of Andy Belcher 45.

The Automobile Association would also like to thank the New Zealand Automobile Association for their assistance in verifying information for the Practical Matters section of this book.

Contributors
Page Layout: Phil Barfoot Researcher: (Practical Matters): Lesley Allard Indexer: Marie Lorimer
This edition updated by: Michael Mellor Managing Editors: Apostrophe S Limited

Dear Essential Traveller

Your comments, opinions and recommendations are very important to us. So please help us to improve our travel guides by taking a few minutes to complete this simple questionnaire.

You do not need a stamp (unless posted outside the UK). If you do not want to cut this page from your guide, then photocopy it or write your answers on a plain sheet of paper.

Send to: **The Editor, AA World Travel Guides, FREEPOST SCE 4598, Basingstoke RG21 4GY.**

Your recommendations...

We always encourage readers' recommendations for restaurants, nightlife or shopping – if your recommendation is used in the next edition of the guide, we will send you a *FREE* AA *Essential* **Guide** of your choice. Please state below the establishment name, location and your reasons for recommending it.

_____

_____

_____

_____

Please send me **AA *Essential*** _____

(*see list of titles inside the front cover*)

About this guide...

Which title did you buy?

AA *Essential* _____

Where did you buy it? _____

When? <u>m m</u> / <u>y y</u>

Why did you choose an AA *Essential* Guide? _____

_____

_____

_____

_____

Did this guide meet your expectations?

Exceeded ☐   Met all ☐   Met most ☐   Fell below ☐

Please give your reasons _____

_____

_____

_____

continued on next page...

Were there any aspects of this guide that you particularly liked? _____

_____

_____

_____

Is there anything we could have done better? _____

_____

_____

_____

_____

About you...

Name (*Mr/Mrs/Ms*) _____

Address _____

_____

_____ Postcode _____

Daytime tel nos _____

Which age group are you in?

Under 25 ☐ 25–34 ☐ 35–44 ☐ 45–54 ☐ 55–64 ☐ 65+ ☐

How many trips do you make a year?

Less than one ☐ One ☐ Two ☐ Three or more ☐

Are you an AA member? Yes ☐ No ☐

About your trip...

When did you book? <u>m m</u> / <u>y y</u>   When did you travel? <u>m m</u> / <u>y y</u>

How long did you stay? _____

Was it for business or leisure? _____

Did you buy any other travel guides for your trip?

If yes, which ones? _____

_____

Thank you for taking the time to complete this questionnaire. Please send
it to us as soon as possible, and remember, you do not need a stamp
(*unless posted outside the UK*).

Happy Holidays!

The Atlas

Acknowledgements
All pictures are from AA World Travel Library with contributions from the following photographers:
Andy Belcher: rock carving at Lake Taupo
Paul Kenward: Maori dancer, Wellington at night, Kelly Tarlton's Underwater World, illuminated
fountains in Christchurch
Steve Watkins: Cycad

The Automobile Association
www.theAA.com
The Automobile Association's website offers comprehensive and up-to-the-minute information covering AA-approved hotels, guest houses and B&Bs, restaurants and pubs in the UK; airport parking, insurance, European breakdown cover, European motoring advice, a ferry planner, European route planner, overseas fuel prices, a bookshop and much more.

The Foreign and Commonwealth Office
Country advice, traveller's tips, before you
go information, checklists and more.
www.fco.gov.uk

Official Tourism NZ
www.purenz.com

GENERAL
UK Passport Service
www.ukpa.gov.uk

Health Advice for Travellers
www.doh.gov.uk/traveladvice

UK Travel Insurance Directory
www.uktravelinsurancedirectory.co.uk

BBC – Holiday
www.bbc.co.uk/holiday

The Full Universal Currency Converter
www.xe.com/ucc/full.shtml

Flying with Kids
www.flyingwithkids.com

www.dayout.co.nz
www.ki-wi.co.nz
www.tourist-offices.org.uk/New_Zealand
www.heli-flights.co.nz

TRAVEL
Flights and Information
www.airnewzealand.com
www.cheapflights.co.uk
www.thisistravel.co.uk
www.ba.com
www.worldairportguide.com

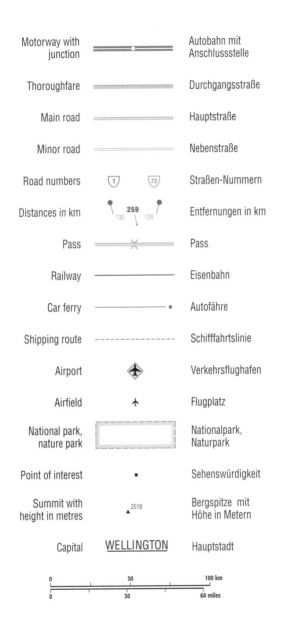

Motorway with junction		Autobahn mit Anschlussstelle
Thoroughfare		Durchgangsstraße
Main road		Hauptstraße
Minor road		Nebenstraße
Road numbers	1 73	Straßen-Nummern
Distances in km	130 259 129	Entfernungen in km
Pass		Pass
Railway		Eisenbahn
Car ferry		Autofähre
Shipping route		Schifffahrtslinie
Airport		Verkehrsflughafen
Airfield		Flugplatz
National park, nature park		Nationalpark, Naturpark
Point of interest		Sehenswürdigkeit
Summit with height in metres	▲ 2518	Bergspitze mit Höhe in Metern
Capital	<u>WELLINGTON</u>	Hauptstadt

```
0          50          100 km
0          30          60 miles
```

Maps © Mairs Geographischer Verlag / Falk Verlag, 73751 Ostfildern

A

Three Kings
Islands

Cape
Reinga
Cape Maria
van Diemen

Ninety

Mile

Beach

*Ahipara
Bay*

Tauroa Point

Herekino

Mitimiti

B

Te Paki
311
Kapowairau
Te Hapua

North Cape

Te Kao

1

89
Pokenui

Awanui

Kaitaia

Ahipara

Kohukohu

Rawene

Opononi
Omapere

*Great
Exhibition
Bay*

North Island

*Rangaunu
Bay*
Merita

*Doubtless
Bay*

Mangonui

Cape Karikari

Karikari Peninsula

Taupo Bay

Mangamuka

87

Okaihau

Taheke

*Hokianga
Harbour*
774

Waipoua
Kauri
Forest

C

Cavalli
Islands

Matauri

61

10 48

Kaeo

Kerikeri
Waimate
North
Ohaeawai

8

12 58

Wai

Paihi

Moerewa Kaw

Kaikohe

Northland Forest P

Awarua

Parakao

Maungat

Kaihu

87

12

Dargaville

Baylys Beach

Te Kopuru

Taingaehe

T a s m a n

S e a

Tok

Ru

North Head

Sou

P A C I F I C

Islands
ic and
me Park
ape Brett

O C E A N

Home Point
Whangaruru
Harbour
Poor
Knights Islands
Whananaki
hakapara
Ngunguru
urangi *Ngunguru Bay*

ngarei
Parua
Bay Whangarei Heads
hara Bream Head
Bream
Bay Hen and
aka Chicken Islands
14 Waipu

oa Brynderwyn
aturoto Mangawhai
Kaiwaka
27

Little Barrier
Island
722
Port Fitzroy
627
Great Barrier
Island

Tryphena

4

Port
Albert Wellsford
Cape Rodney
Leigh
Hauraki
1 Warkworth
Kawau I.
16 Mahurangi Port
Puhoi Mahurangi West **Gulf** Jackson
Tavern Waiwera
kapa Orewa *Hauraky*
sville Dairy *Gulf* Whangaahei
Flat Whangaparoa Whangaahei
auku Albany **Maritime Park**
ai Beach Kumeu Takapuna Waiheke I.
AUCKLAND Coromandel
Waitakere Onetangi
Piha Howick Ponui I. Whitianga
Maraetai Cooks Beach
ekare Orere Point Coroglen
Huia *Manukau* Papatoetoe Tapu
Harbour Manukau
Matakawa Papakura Kaiaua Firth
Clarks Beach Bombay of *Thames*
Pukekohe *Thames* Kopu
Waiuku Tuakau Pokeno
Port **126** Mangatarata Waitakaruru
Waikato Glen Te Kauwhata Tirohia
Murray *Lake* 27 **210**
Waikare Paeroa
Naike Aroha

Colville Channel

Cuvier I.

Great Mercury I.
Red Mercury I.
892
Port
Charles

Kuatonu *Mercury Bay*
103
Cathedral
Cove Slipper Island
Hot
Water Beach
59 Coromandel
846 Peninsula
Pauanui
Coromandel
Forest Park
Whangamata

25
Waihi
Waihi Mayor Island
Beach
953
Matakana Island
Tauranga Harbour

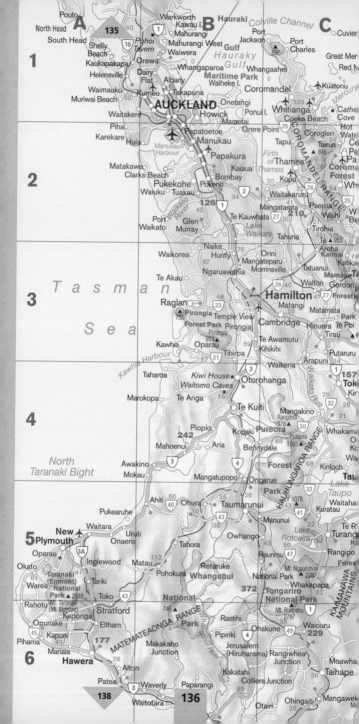

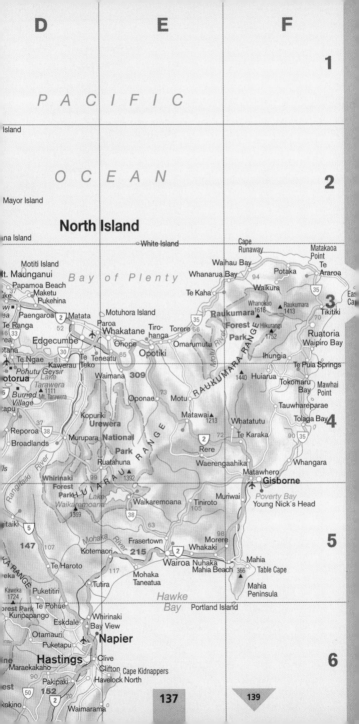

P A C I F I C

Island

O C E A N

Mayor Island

North Island

na Island

White Island

Cape Runaway

Matakaoa Point

Te Araroa

Waihau Bay

Whanarua Bay

Potaka

Motiti Island

Bay of Plenty

Whangara Bay

94

Waikura

Papamoa Beach

Mt. Maunganui

Maketu

Pukehina

Te Kaha

35

Eas
Ca

ke
37

wi
ea

Paengaroa

2

Matata

Te Ranga

52

Paroa

Motuhora Island

Raukumara

Whangao

Raukumara
1413

Tikitiki

70

33

Whakatane

Tiro-
hanga

Torere

66

35

Forest

1618
Hikurangi
1752

Ruatoria
Waipiro Bay

Edgecumbe

Ohope

Omarumutu

Park

otaha

Te Ngae

81

Kawerau

Iteko

Te Teneatu

Opotiki

Ihungia

Te Pula Springs

Pohutu
Geysir

Waimana

309

Motu

1440

Huiarua

Tokomaru
Bay

Mawhai
Point

otorua

Lake
Tarawera

1111
Mt. Tarawera

Oponae

73

Matawai

Tauwhareparae

5
Burried
Village

Kopuriki

Urewera

1213

Whatatutu

Tolaga Bay

apu

37

National

Te Karaka

90

35

Reporoa

38

Murupara

Park

72

Rere

Broadlands

Ruatahuna

2

Waerengaahika

Whangara

Is

Whirinaki

1392

Matawhero

Gisborne

Forest

Lake

Waikaremoana

Tiniroto

Muriwai

Poverty Bay

itaiki

Park

1369

Waikaremoana

105

Young Nick's Head

5

147

107

38

63

98

Morere

KA RANGE

Mohaka River

Frasertown

Whakaki

Mahia

Kotemaori

215

2

Wairoa

Nuhaka

Mahia Beach

366

Table Cape

Te Haroto

117

Mahia
Peninsula

Kaweka
1724

Puketitiri

Tutira

Mohaka
Taneatua

*Hawke
Bay*

Portland Island

rest Park

Te Pohue

Whirinaki

Kuripapango

Eskdale

Bay View

Otamauri

Puketapu

Napier

ine

Hastings

Clive

Maraekakaho

Clifton

Cape Kidnappers

90

Pakipaki

Havelock North

50

152

2

139

okino

Waimarama

A 136

1
New Plymouth
Waitara
Pukea
Uruti
Onaero
Oparau
Okato
3A
Inglewood
Matau
Po
Taranaki (Egmont) National Park
Tariki
Cape Egmont Warea
Rahotu
▲2518
Toko
43
Stratford
Mt. Taranaki (Mt. Egmont)
45
Kaponga
Opunake
Eltham
Kapuni
177
MATEMATEA
Pihama
43
28
Manaia
Alton
Hawera
Patea
3 Wa
Waito

2
T a s m a n

S e a

3
So
Taranak

Cape Farewell   Farewell Spit
Whanganui Inlet   Puponga
Pakawa
South Island
Paturau River
1213▲
Collingwood
Golden Bay
Cape Stephens
Kahurangi Point
Mt. Stevens
Takaka
60
Separation Point
Totaranui
D'Urville Island
Kahurangi
Devil River Peak
85
Abel Tasman
729▲**Marlborough**
4
TASMAN 1775▲ Upper Takaka
National Park
Marahau
Sounds Maritime Park
National
Kaiteriteri
Tasman Bay
Pepin I.
French Pass
971
(Mt. Stokes)
MOUNTAINS
Motueka
▲1203
1623
Mariri
Tasman
Wakapuaka
79
Portage
Pli
Arapawa I.
Po
Karamea
Park
Ngatimoti
Mount
Rai Valley
Kenepuru Head
1826
Upper Moutere
60
Nelson
6
Richmond
Havelock
Picton
Mt. Kendall
48 61
Mapua
Richmond
Cape Terawhiti
Little Wanganui
1811
Tapawera
Kohatu
30
Wakefield
Forest Park
1760
31
Tuamarina
WELLING
5
Mt. Owen
Korere
Belgrove
RICHMOND RANGE
Renwick
Cloudy Bay
1875
Hope Saddle
40
Wairau River
Blenheim
Strait
Owen River
6
Kawatiri
Kikiwa
63
Wairau Valley
✈*Wine Area*
444
Rotoroa
Murchison
26
Pinnacle
2120
102
1780
Seddon
Saltworks
Lake Rotoroa
St. Arnaud
Te Arowhenua
70
Cape Campbell
Lake Rotoiti
Ward
Paenga
Nelson Lakes
Tapuae-o-Uenuku
2885
Awatere River
65
2339
National Park
Molesworth
Kekerengu
6
Springs Junction
Mt Una
2301
INLAND KAIKOURA RANGE
Clarence
SEAWARD KAIKOURA RANGE
Moruia Springs
1945▲Mt. Clara
Clarence River
2174
2609
62
323
Lewis Pass
2885
Manakau
350
Hanmer Forest Park
141
138
1
Kaikoura
Hanmer Springs
70
110
Kaikoura Peninsula

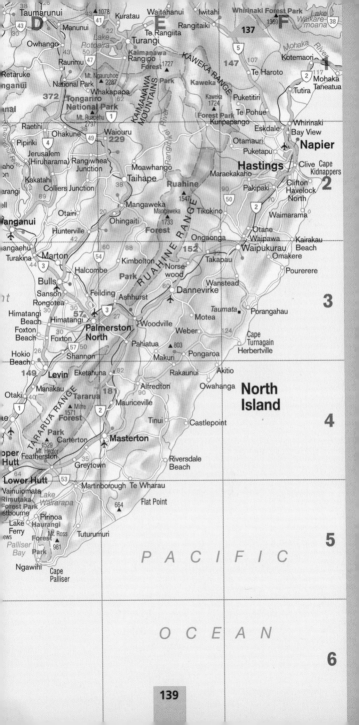

D   **E**   **F**

Taumarunui
1078
Kuratau
Waitahanui
Iwitahi
Whirinaki Forest Park
Lake Waikaremoana

Manunui
Rangitaiki
Rangitikei
1369
137
38

Owhango
Turangi
Mohaka River

Raurimu
Lake Rotoaira
Kaimanawa
Rangipo
Forest
1727
Kotemaori
107
Te Haroto
Kaweka Range
147

Retaruke
National Park
Whakapapa
Mt Ngauruhoe 2287
Kaweka Forest Park
1724
Puketitiri
Te Pohue
Tutira
Mohaka
Taneatua
1

372
Tongariro National Park
Mt Ruapehu 2797
Kaimanawa Mountains
Kunpapango
Eskdale
Whirinaki
Bay View
Napier

Raetihi
Ohakune
Waiouru 229
Otamauri
Puketapu
Hastings
Clive Cape
Kidnappers

Pipiriki
Rangiwhea Junction
Moawhango
Maraekakaho
Pakipaki
Clifton
Havelock
North
2

Jerusalem (Hiruharama)
Taihape
Ruahine
1547
90
50
Waimarama

Kakatahi
Colliers Junction
Mangaweka
Mangaweka 1733
Tikokino
Otane
Waipawa
Kairakau Beach

Wanganui
Otairi
Ohingaiti
Forest
Ongaonga
Waipukurau
152
Omakere
Pourerere

Hunterville
Kimbolton
Norse wood
Takapau
3

Turakina
Marton
54
Norsewood
Wanstead
Taumata
Porangahau

Bulls
Halcombe
Park
Dannevirke
Motea
Cape Turnagain
Herbertville

Sanson
Rongotea
Feilding
Ashhurst
60
Woodville
Weber 803
124

Himatangi Beach
Himatangi
57
Palmerston North
27
Pahiatua
Pongaroa

Foxton Beach
Foxton
50
Shannon
Makuri
Rakaunui
Akitio

Hokio Beach
149
Levin
Eketahuna 82
Alfredton
Owahanga

Otaki
Manakau
Tararua Range
181
Mauriceville
North Island
4

Mitre 1571
Tararua Forest Park
Tinui
Castlepoint

Upper Hutt
Carterton
Masterton
Riversdale Beach

Featherston
Mt Hector 1529
Greytown

Lower Hutt
53
Martinborough
Te Wharau

Wainuiomata
Rimutaka Forest Park
Eastbourne
Lake Wairarapa
Flat Point 664

Lake Ferry
Pirinoa
Haurangi
Tuturumuri
5

Mt Ross 981
Forest Park

Ngawihi
Cape Palliser
P A C I F I C

O C E A N
6

	A	B	C
1			
2			
3			
4			
5			
6			

South Island

Kahurangi Pt

Kah

TAS

Karamea
Bight

Tasman

Mokohinui

Hector
Granity   Old C
Waimangaroa   Mines
Carters
Beach
Cape Foulwind   Westport Lyell

Sea

Charleston *Old Gold*
Town
Inangahua

Paen
Victoria
Mt. Vict
1640

Punakaiki Paparoa
Nat. P.   Reefton
▲1531
Pancake Rocks
and Blowholes   Old Gold
Mine Maru
Barrytown   Forest   Par
Black-   Ikamatua
Runanga   ball

Greymouth   Ahaura
Paroa   Ngahere   Spring
Shantytown   Still-   Junctio
Kumara   water   Moana
Junction   Kumara   *Lake*
Mt. Ajax
Hokitika   *Brunner*   1832
Kaniere   Inchbonnie   Mount Long
Forest
Lake Sum
Ross   Kokatahi   Arthur's Pass
Old Coldfield   Otira ▲2088   Park
Lake   Arthur's Pass
Kaniere   Arthur's Pass **National Park**
Mt. Murchison
Abut Head   ▲2204   2400 *Ski Area*
Harihari   Craigieburn
Forest Park
Okarito   **532**   ▲2644 *Lake* ▲2195
Whataroa   Mt. Whitcombe   *Coleridge*
Westland *Lake* Franz-Josef   ▲2545 Mt. Arrowsmith   Lake
Gillespies *Matheson* 97 Glacier   2865   Coleridge   Oxford
Beach   ■Franz-Josef   2795 *Lake*
Fox Glacier Fox Glacier *Glacier*   *Heron*   Sprinfield
Mount Cook   ▲2330 *Ski* Sheffield
▲3117   *Area*
3754 **National**   The Thumbs   Alford Mount Hutt
2545   Hakatere   Forest   Hororata Darfiel
Jacobs Mount Cook/Aoraki   Methven
River Mount **Park**   Mount Rolle
111 **Cook** *Lilybank*   Somers   Dunsandel
Mt. Hooker **Park**   Ben Mc Leod   77 Doyles
2652   ▲1951
▲2644 *Lake* *Ski Area*   Montaito   47 Chertsey
Tekapo   ▲2332   96 South
2499   Mayfield   1 Pindarves
57   Sherwood   72
Mt. Huxley *Lake* *Lake*   Downs   Tinwald **162** Wakanui Elles
▲2499 *Pukaki* Tekapo   Arundel Maronan   **Ashburton**
80   8   Hakatere
Ski Area   Fairlie   Geraldine   50 Lowcliffe
Twizel   Burke   79 Orari
Mt. Saint Mary   **143** Pass   **140** Pleasant Clandeboye
2332 ▲   Chamberlain   Point Temuka

Kumara

PAPAROA RANGE

PUKETERA

Waimakariri River

Rakaia River

Rangitata R.

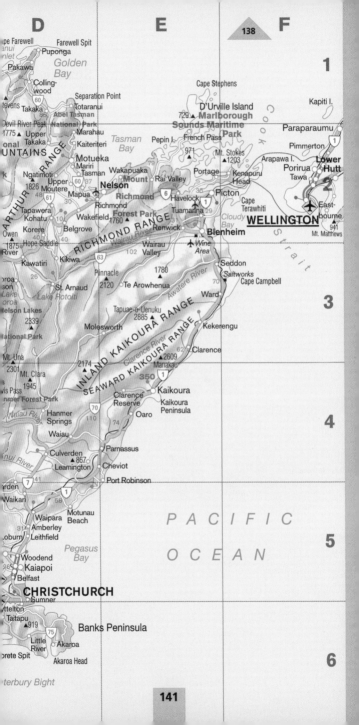

1

pe Farewell   Farewell Spit
anui   Puponga
nlet
Pakawa   *Golden Bay*

Cape Stephens

Kapiti I.

evens   Colling-wood   Separation Point
Takaka   60   Totaranui
evil River Peak   *Abel Tasman*
1775 ▲ Upper   *National Park*   Marahau
onal   Kaiteriteri

D'Urville Island
729 ▲ **Sounds Maritime**
Park
Pepin I.   French Pass
971
Mt. Stokes
▲1203

Paraparaumu

Pimmerton

Arapawa I.   **Lower**
Kenapuru   Porirua   **Hutt**
Head   Tawa

UNTAINS

Tasman Bay

Motueka
Mariri   Tasman   Wakapuaka
Ngatimoti   Upper   **Mount**   Rai Valley
1826 ▲ Moutere   **Nelson**
48   Mapua   **Richmond**

2

Portage

Picton

Cape
Terawhiti   **WELLINGTON**
East-bourne
941
Mt. Matthews

Tapawera   Richmond
Kohatu   **Forest Park**
Owen   Korere   Wakefield 1760
1875 ▲ Belgrove
Hope Saddle   40
River

Havelock
Tuamarina   29
Renwick   **Blenheim**

Cloudy Bay

Kawatiri

Kikiwa   63   Wairau   *Wine*   Area
Valley
102

Seddon
Saltworks   Cape Campbell

oroa-   Pinnacle   1780
son   St. Arnaud   2120   Te Arowhenua
Lake   *Lake Rotoiti*
oroa
elson Lakes
2339

Ward

3

Molesworth

Tapuae-o-Uenuku
2885

Kekerengu

National Park

Mt. Una
2301
Mt. Clara
1945

2174

2609
Manakau
350

Clarence
Clarence
Reserve   Kaikoura
Oaro   Kaikoura
Peninsula

is Pass
nmer Forest Park   70
Waiau Rv   Hanmer
Springs   110
Waiau   74

4

nui River   Culverden
▲ 867
Leamington   Cheviot

Parnassus

arden
Waikari   7   141   1
58

Port Robinson

P A C I F I C

Waipara   Motunau
Beach
Amberley
oburn   Leithfield   *Pegasus Bay*

O C E A N

5

Woodend
Kaiapoi
Belfast
CHRISTCHURCH
Sumner

ttelton
Taitapu   ▲919   75   Banks Peninsula
Little
River   Akaroa

6

rete Spit   Akaroa Head

terbury Bight

A   **B**   **C**

1

South Island

Cascade Point

Jackson Head

Jackson Ba

T a s m a n

S e a

2

Awarua Point

Big Bay

Yates Point

Mount A

National 30

Milford Sound

2000 ▲ Mt. Tutoko ▲ 2746

Park

Sutherland Sound

1692 ▲ ✈ Milford Sound

▲ 2518

Bligh Sound

Mitre Peak

George Sound

▲ 1472

Sutherland Falls ■

▲ 2502 Glenorchy Skippers

3

Caswell Sound

2036 ▲

Mt. Mc Dougall

Charles Sound

Thompson Sound

Secretary Island

Lake Te Anau

94

6A 53

Arro

Fiordland

Doubtful Sound

Mt. Lyall

▲ 1905

Te Anau Downs

Jane Peak ▲ 2035

Queenstown Frankt

Dagg Sound

Glowworm Caves

Lake Wakatipu

Kingston

National

Lake Manapouri

Te Anau

1598 ▲

The Key

Athol

Deep Cove

121

Oreti R.

EYRE MOUNTAINS

Five Rivers

4

Breaksea Sound

West Arm

Manapouri

94

78

Resolution Island

▲ 1768

Mossburn

226

Lumsden

Dusky Sound

Lake Monowai

Monowai

70

Ardluss

Lintley Ki

Park

Avondale

50

94 Cr

Dipton West Dipton

59

Waiau River

Ohai

95

6

Riversdale

Mandevill

Cape Providence

▲ 1049

Caroline Peak ▲ 1722

Nightcaps

96

Wreys Bush

Centre Bush

Chalky Inlet

CAMERON MTS.

Clifden

Orawia

Otautau

Drummond

Winton

Wilsons Crossing

Preservation Inlet

Puysegur Point

Lake Poteriteri

Lake Hauroko

Tuatapere

Fairfax

Hedgeh

Edendale

Te Waeae Bay

Orepuki

Thornbury

99 87

Wallace

Corne-ville

Wynd Gle

5

Solander I.

Colac Bay Riverton town

31

Wood lands

1

22

Invercargill

Gorge Road

F o v e a u x   S t r a i t

Bluff Tiwai Point

Toetoes Bay Fe

Codfish Island

Mt. Anglem ▲ 980

Halfmoon Bay (Oban)

Ruapuke Island

Mason Bay

Paterson Inlet

Shelter Point

6

Mt. Allen ▲ 750

Big South Cape I.

Pearl Island

Stewart Island

142

South Cape

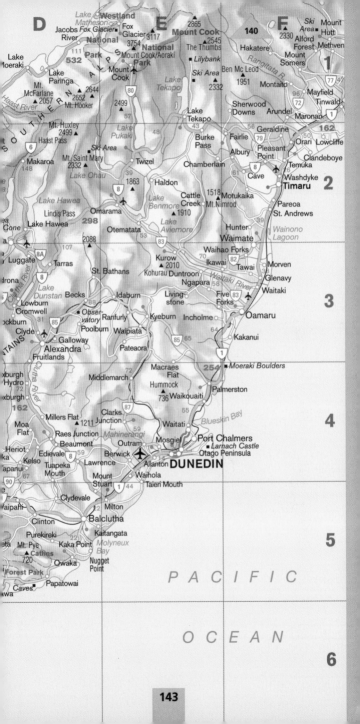

Lake Matheson
Westland
Jacobs Fox Glacier
River
Fox
National
Glacier
532
Mount Cook
2865
Park
111
3117
140
Mount Cook/Aoraki
3754
Park
National
Mount Cook
Park
2545
Lilybank
The Thumbs
Hakatere
Ski Area
140
2330
Ski
Mount
Area
Hutt
Alford Methven
Forest
Mount
Somers
1

Lake Moeraki
Lake Paringa
Mt. McFarlane
2057
2644
2652
Mt. Hooker
2499
80
Mount Cook
Ben Mc Leod
1951
Montaito
Sherwood Downs
Arundel
Maronan
96
72
Mayfield
Tinwald
77 47
Lake Tekapo
Lake Tekapo
43
Geraldine
Fairlie
Albury
79
Pleasant Point
Orari
Clandeboye
Lowcliffe
50
162

SOUTHERN
Mt. Huxley
2499
Haast Pass
Haast River
6
Makaroa
148
Mt. Saint Mary
2332
Ski Area
Twizel
1863
8
Haldon
Chamberlain
Cave
8
61
Washdyke
Temuka
Timaru
Pareoa
St. Andrews
Wainono Lagoon
2

ALPS
Lake Pukaki
Lake Ohau
48
Lake Benmore
Cattle Creek
1518
Mt. Nimrod
Motukaika
39
Hunter
Waimate
2

Cone
Lake Hawea
Lindis Pass
Lake Hawea
298
Omarama
2088
Otematata
Lake Aviemore
53
83
Waihao Forks
Ikawai
70
Waitaki River
82
Tawai
Morven
Glenavy
Waitaki
39

Luggage
8A
Tarras
107
Kurow
2010
Kohurau
Duntroon
Ngapara
Five Forks
83
Oamaru
3

Irona
8
Lake Dunstan
Lowburn
Cromwell
31
Clyde
85
Beaufort
88
St. Bathans
Becks
Idaburn
Obser-
vatory
Ranfurly
Poolburn
Waipiata
Living-
stone
Kyeburn
Incholme
85
65
64
Kakanui

MOUNTAINS
Alexandra
Fruitlands
Galloway
Pateaora
Macraes Flat
Hummock
736
Waikouaiti
254
Moeraki Boulders
Palmerston
1

xburgh
Hydro
72
xburgh
162
Moa Flat
Millers Flat
1211
Clarks Junction
87
Raes Junction
Mahinerangi
59
Beaumont
Outram
Mosgiel
Waitati
55
Blueskin Bay
Port Chalmers
Larnach Castle
Otago Peninsula
4

Heriot
ka
Kelso
apanui
90
67
Edievale
8
Tuapeka Mouth
Lawrence
Berwick
Allanton
DUNEDIN
Waihola

Clydevale
Mount Stuart
1
44
Taieri Mouth

aipahi
Clinton
Milton
Balclutha
Kaitangata
Molyneux Bay
5

Purekireki
Mt. Pye
720
Cathlins
Owaka
22
Kaka Point
Nugget Point

eta
Forest Park
Caves
Papatowai
awa

PACIFIC
6

OCEAN

143